ONE EYE CRYING, ONE EYE LAUGHING

A Transylvanian Tasmanian story

Shirley Castley

Almost everything in this book is true.

Hungarian names have often been assigned the correct, accented Hungarian spelling but not always.

Copyright: Shirley Castley

2011

PART ONE: ÉVA

1. Eastern Transylvania   4

2. Northern Transylvania   23

3. Budapest   29

4. Tasmania   82

PART TWO: SHIRLEY

5. Balikpapan, Hobart and Launceston
                                                       89

6. Launceston   128

7. The Trial   153

8. Vienna, Budapest, Transylvania and Bangkok – the blogs   210

9. Hobart: A Farewell too hard to bear

                                                     290

Photos   291

PART ONE: ÉVA

1. Eastern Transylvania

1926: Miklósvár Transylvania

The six year old sat in her window watching the snow move gently to the ground far below. For days now the snow had been falling and she had not been able to play outside with any of the children who came to her from the village. She was warm and comfortable and looking forward with an eagerness which squeezed at her to Christmas which was in three weeks and to her seventh birthday which was in four weeks. She had cut out little pieces of paper with carefully written numbers on them and every day she tore one of them into small pieces so that the diminishing pile added to her happiness as it became smaller. She had very dark hair, not quite black, and a grave intelligent face which reflected a rich, somewhat smug, inner life based on her own assessment of her abilities, which were boundless. This night she had a plan.

Her parents were holding a ball downstairs. The house itself, a large manor house which had been a fortified keep some centuries ago, was full with guests, some of whom were staying the night or a few days and some of whom had arrived by carriage or car and would be staying in some sort of lodgings in nearby villages or towns. The nearest large town was Brassó but this would only be reachable by those with cars. She didn't really know any of this. Mainly what she knew was excitement and anticipation. Her plan was to wait until the noise levels became strong and absorbent of her movements and to creep halfway down the staircase and watch the dancing and the colour. She would imagine how it would be for her when she was old enough to dress up in beautiful sumptuous clothing and truly participate.

Meanwhile she had to wait.

She kicked her legs, swung her legs, snuggled up to herself. The fire in the heater over in the corner of her bedroom had died down and, although the tiles were probably still too hot to touch the room was beginning to chill and the windows to fog slightly. She was not bored at all. In fact she was keeping watch at the window in the faint hope of seeing angels again. This morning when she had woken she had heard a quiet tinkling in the air. She listened for a while and couldn't quite decide where it was coming from. The bedroom was quite cool and it had snowed overnight she thought. She wriggled around in her bed wondering if she should go and wake her parents. She knew they would not be pleased what with late nights, house guests and all that. She lay there for a while and the tinkling continued intermittently. She twisted her head to look at the faint dawn beginning to lighten the sky outside and then she saw it. Or rather she saw them.

Hanging down outside here window were the tips of long silvery angels' wings, a good ten or twelve of them, swaying slightly and occasionally glinting and shaking. She rushed out of bed and raced to the window and tried to look up so that she could see their faces but she was unable to see more than a foot or so. Nevertheless she held very still and watched the wings dangling and jangling in the tiny breeze which she could also hear in the pine trees. This was something she had never ever seen before although her parents talked of angels at Christmas and the priest in the church also preached of angels taking care of people, particularly children. She had never heard of angels sitting on rooftops and dangling their wings so that they shimmered and tinkled. She had always known she was special and she thought this was something extraordinary which the angels had done just for her in the morning with no-one else to see. She crept back into her bed and tried to watch intently to make sure that she didn't miss any of the movements and to see if they would fly away. In spite of her resolve she had succumbed to the warmth of the bed and the early hour and drifted back off to sleep. When she woke again later the angels had gone and it was full light and she was very angry with herself. She swore that it would not happen again hence her evening vigil was doubly engrossing.

It was very dark outside by now and even if the angels returned she wasn't sure if she would be able to see them. Maybe they just came in the mornings? She wondered what time it was. The noise from the ball downstairs had been increasing but now it seemed a bit quieter which was unusual. The guests who were not staying in the house had arrived early and the balls usually got underway fairly briskly while it was still dusk as they drew to a close before midnight to allow for travel. However the music and the sounds of occasional laughter and the muted battering of multiple shoes dancing and moving about was consistent and escalating as the night proceeded. She could hear music still but just very quietly. She wondered what on earth was happening. It was time to go downstairs.

She crept over the rugs to the door and quietly opened it expecting a huge swirl of noise and music but it was surprisingly muted. Along to the end of the bedroom hallway and to the door which opened onto the staircase. This door was slightly ajar so she squeezed through it without moving it. She stepped onto the stone staircase which curved around from the top floor to the main floor and then descended to the vaulted cellars below. There were some candles burning in the wall niches so she had no trouble stepping lightly down to her favourite watching spot. Still there were only quiet talky voices coming to her with none of the jingly rhythmic music and shouts of laughter which was usual for such occasions. She strained to listen and thought she could hear her father's voice.

"It's been coming for years now and ...[inaudible]... they will ...[mumble]....go to the vineyard [inaudible]"

Her grandfather's voice next. Her grandfather was a teacher like her father although they both were serving army officers as well. She was surprised to hear her grandfather speaking Hungarian. He rarely, if ever, spoke anything other than Latin which he was teaching her when he wasn't working.

"This is our home." Her grandfather was speaking more loudly and she could hear him quite clearly. "We have been here for generations. If we leave we will never ever be able to return. The roughnecks and the envious will take it all, not to preserve it or to treasure it but to piss on it."

She had never heard her grandfather swear, not even in Latin and she became just a little frightened. Other voices now but she decided not to listen anymore as it was all too confusing. Then she heard her mother.

"We have two small children, one is just a baby and we can't risk [mumble]...."

She was mystified and just the smallest bit frightened. She could understand the words, sort of, and they seemed to hold a menace which unsettled her and made her try and not think too hard about the meaning. She screwed up her eyes.

"Évike what are you doing there…?" Her mother had come through the door which opened onto the stairwell. "You know you should be in bed my darling. I was just coming to kiss you and make sure you were asleep and yet here you are.."

Her mother looked quite gorgeous. Her blond hair was piled up in the new fashion and her clothing was elegant and she wafted a subtle perfume.

"Sorry Mami. I was spying on the ball but there's nothing much happening."

"Come on darling I will take you back to bed." Her mother was never angry but right now she didn't even seem all that concerned about her night time exploits. She was distracted and seemed tense.

They walked back up the staircase and her mother tucked her tightly back into bed. "How long now till Christmas?"

she whispered. "And how long till your birthday?" This was a little game they started playing, usually in early November, but Éva (for that was her name) was not in the mood. "What were Father and Grandfather talking about to the other people Mami?" "Nothing to worry you Évike, it's just some grumbling about things that grownups grumble about."

"But Mami, I heard them say that we have to leave here." Her mother pursed her lips. She knew that this was an intelligent, sensitive child who would brood and think and shake her small amount of information until it made sense. "Well yes we might have to go to the vineyard for a while. Things are a bit unsettled with the Romanians and we just might need to sort of lay low for a while. Don't worry Évie, we will talk about it all when we know more. I'm sorry you heard what you heard but it will all turn out all right. You must not worry."

Her mother knew that this would not do the trick but it was enough for tonight and Éva closed her eyes, then said "Mami I love you and I love Father and I love Grandfather and I love baby András and Christmas will be soon. We will be here for Christmas and my birthday won't we?"

"Yes darling. Probably we will just go for a short trip to the vineyard in March like we do every year and then come straight back home."

Éva slept then and did not hear the hustle and bustle of the guests' departures.

1927: Miklósvár to Nagyvárad

The family (Lajos Gyenge senior, Lajos Gyenge junior, Piroska Gyenge, Éva Gyenge and András Gyenge) had left early in the morning as it was a very long drive to the vineyard in Nagyvárad over poor roads which had been used only by horses, carts and carriages for the centuries of human settlement. Their car was large and comfortable but could not move fast or evenly over the rutted, wet and muddy roads. Occasionally they had to stop completely if they came across another vehicle or even a horse and cart as there was so little room. Given the snow melt and the freezing conditions this was rare so they were able to manage something a bit better than horse pace. It was about 400 kilometres and they stopped overnight in Segesvár at a small hotel having covered less than half of the route. Baby András was fractious and noisy and they had not had a very restful time in the car. He was even noisier through the night and, as none of them were used to sharing space with him, very little sleep was to be had. They were almost glad of the need for another very early start.

Following a breakfast of rice pudding and milk (for Éva) they reset out on their journey. Éva snuggled down into the blankets on the back seat hoping for some dozing time. She contemplated her adventure a few days back.

Again it had been early morning and it was the day after the family conference when her Father had sat her on his knee and told her that they might not come back to Miklósvár for quite some time. He had been loving and even a bit funny but she could feel the hurt bubbling around her and through her parents' calm and reassuring manner. They had to tell her for otherwise she would have loudly and often asked why they were packing up most of their clothing and furniture to be transported to them later.

It had not snowed for a week although it was very cold. No-one from her family was out of bed yet although there would be some people in the cellars and kitchens and probably the fields. There were always people being busy somewhere with horses or cooking or bringing wood in or doing the very many things which were needed to keep the house and the farmland running smoothly. The house was situated in a very gentle valley with woodlands arising in the near hills and the area watered from the Ort River which was small but reliable. She knew that their house also had a well in the cellars which was fed by the Ort which was used for convenience. She was not usually allowed in the cellars as it was a place of work and she might get in the way or even hurt herself.

She knew that they were leaving soon and she wanted to spend some time just by herself saying goodbye even though she had received multiple reassurances that they would return.

Again, as she had on the night of the ball, she crept downstairs and, instead of turning towards the main living rooms, she went out towards the side door which led to the outside privy. If spotted she could use this as an excuse although the family mainly used chamber pots in the Winter months. She knew that her father was planning to install a flushing water closet but supposed that this would not happen now.

She opened the heavy door and went down the steps into the clear freezing morning. She had rugged up in her warm woolen coat and scarf and her second best gloves. She walked past the brick privy with its three cubicles and pushed open the gate which led to the back side of the house and to the river.

Once through the gate she turned and looked at her lovely house. Although there were many pine trees in the main garden it was not so well wooded on this side of the house but there were fruit trees and berries (if you knew where to look), some of them wild and self sown. She had a notion that some raspberries might be nice although she wasn't sure if there were any at this time of year.

Her feet crunched on the frosty ground as she walked up the slight hill away from the house. Her breath made small clouds as she walked. She spotted some brambly looking underbrush closer to the river and thought that was a likely finding spot. When she got closer she saw that there were some bright orangey coloured berries or small fruit – not raspberries but they might be tasty. She had never been this far from the house by herself before. She reached out with her gloved hand to pick one of the brightly coloured morsels and then stopped with her hand in mid air as she saw movement on the other side of the thicket.

Was it a farm labourer or someone who would tell her parents what she had been up to? She started to turn when she heard a snuffling sound. A large brown shape rose up from the thicket less than a metre away from her. Eyes peered at her through the entwined branches and she realized that she was face to face with a big brown bear who had obviously also been attracted to the winter berries. She was a brave little girl and knew better than to react in a way which could startle the bear. She had not been told this but all her instincts kept her from making any sudden movements. She needed to get back to the gate near the privy but to do that she really needed to turn around. She was extremely reluctant to turn around as she thought her only hope was to keep the bear in her sights.

She couldn't shout or call for help in any way. No-one would, in any case, be likely to hear her. She stepped backwards. The bear did not move but was still on its hind legs looking at her. She took another step backwards and then another. This was risky as the ground was uneven and frosty and she couldn't see where her feet were landing. Her heart was beating quite wildly and she gulped some air. One more step backwards and then the bear suddenly dropped to all fours and began to shuffle away from her. She stayed very still then and waited until she thought it might be safe to turn around and walk as quickly as she could back to the gate, the privies and the safety of the house.

She told no-one of her adventure until after a great deal of time had passed.

It was much, much later when they stopped for something to eat which was just some pork stew and rough bread at a small restaurant but it was enough and, although they talked about stopping somewhere for another night's sleep, it was decided that they should move on. It was dark when they finally entered the outskirts of Nagyvárad and drove through to the hilly vineyards of Vie. The house was warm and welcoming. Fires had been laid and lit and food prepared for them. Éva was too tired to eat and she was tucked into her bed. András had been asleep for some time and, although he set up a complaining wail he too was put to bed in what was to be their home for the next 13 years.

2. Northern Transylvania

It was pretty good. Éva went to school in what was now Oradea, a part of the new Romania. She spoke Hungarian with her family at home but was comfortably bilingual. This later became multilingual as she learnt Latin, French and German at school. Languages came easily to her, perhaps as a result of her grandfather's Latin instruction when she was a toddler.

Her blonde haired, blue eyed mother seemed reasonably content. Why, oh why, thought Éva frequently, did she not inherit these very un-Hungarian features. Why did she have to be her father's child with her olive skin and dark hair? In other respects she was nothing like her father as his almost Mongoloid face, fairly short stature was more akin to Attila and to her brother!

He shaved his head completely, perhaps to look much fiercer, although she only ever knew him as gentle and loving and patient and kind. She was the apple of his eye. The only times she saw him to be emotional or upset, even sometimes angry was at the dinner table. Her mother was in the habit of prodding him to talk about his experiences in the World War. He was always reluctant and she could understand why as the stories he told of misery and cold and hunger in the Italian Alps were almost too much to bear. She knew also that some stories were not for her ears but that her mother would sometimes lead him off to his small study so that they could talk quietly together about unknown horrors. This did not happen often, it was more usual for the dinner table conversations to be laced with allusions that only her mother and father understood. Éva did not know why they didn't just talk of lovely things at dinner, why they had to delve and speak of the past in this way. She later understood what her mother had clearly understood only too well, that to hide feelings about hurt, pain and guilt was to obstruct all emotion and thus create a distortion of relationship with the world and with others. You could not love freely if you could not be tender with your own self.

They also talked incessantly about Miklósvár as it was their shared hurt and loss.

The vineyard flourished and they prospered modestly. They had brought a large number of valuable pieces with them when they fled Miklósvár but most of these were kept in storage, perhaps awaiting the day when they could return.

Éva had many friends as she was intelligent and funny. She had some Romanian friends but mostly Hungarian. The Romanians seemed somehow to resent her which she didn't really understand as they had taken her country – or so her parents said.

Apart from being a very good student in all her subjects she had a truly wonderful experience one day when she was returning from school. It was 1935 or 36. In any case she was a gangly teenager walking home with her friends along one of the narrow streets in Nagyvárad/Oradea. It was about four o'clock and a bright, crisp, cloudless day.

The sky suddenly began to darken and she looked around with her friends. Was it a big cloud or a rain storm approaching? "Éva, Éva, we'd better run." One of her friends shouted. It got darker and darker and they looked up. There was a huge 'thing' beginning to fill up the sky, filling up the whole space between the tops of the houses in the street. It continued to do this, not just gradually darkening but closing up the space like pulling a jumper over your head. The girls screamed loudly, as did many other people in the street. A young soldier, seeing the girls becoming very frightened, said in a voice loud enough to be heard by many of the dislocated people. "It's just a dirigible, could be the Hindenburg. Don't be frightened. It's okay. Nothing is going to happen. It will be gone soon."

The airship by then had completely covered the entire sky and it was pitch black in the street below. Éva had heard of the airships but never realized how huge they might be. She ceased being frightened and became fascinated at the dark obliterating shape overhead. It started to move away and the sky slowly opened up to them again in the same measured way it had closed down a few minutes earlier.

What an experience, she thought. I will never forget this. She wasn't to know right then that there would be other experiences which would push this scenic flight out of her head for many years to come.

3. Budapest

In 1940 The Hungarian Government did a deal with Hitler which 'gave back' parts of Northern Transylvania to Hungary. Hungarian troops rode and marched into Oradea, now Nagyvárad again to scenes of great rejoicing. The Hungarian flags were everywhere, with here and there a small Nazi insignia. Éva and her family were watching, waving and cheering along with everyone else. But their joy was tempered by the fact that Father was rejoining his old World War 1 regiment and he felt that, in order to keep the family safe, they should now move to Budapest. He had sold the vineyard to another Hungarian family and everything was packed ready to go. The upside of this for Éva was that she could attend the University in Budapest which was vastly preferable to attending anything in Transylvania. The standard of education in the Transylvanian

Universities had slipped somewhat during the twenty year period of Romanian rule and she wished to gain a really first class degree in history.

They had purchased a house in the prestigious area of Sashegy on the Buda side with lovely tree lined streets and views over to the Danube and beyond. The move this time was by train, with their furniture and other belongings being sent on separately. The train trip was overnight and Éva settled into her small sleeping compartment quite contentedly. She had not been to Budapest but was looking forward to the move which was a little less hasty and forced that the move from Miklósvár.

"Do you think Father will be allright?" she had asked her Mother expecting and hoping for reassurance. "Yes darling, this war will be over very soon and we will all be together in Budapest until we can return to Miklósvár".

"Do you really think that will ever happen Mami? After all we don't even know who is living there or even if it still stands."

Her Mother grimaced and lit a cigarette. She had asked her doctor if she should give up and he had said "No, no, it is good for you, helping you to relax."

"No we don't know that but once it is returned to us we can do whatever it takes to make it our own again."

Their arrival in Budapest was without incident. Again the streets were somewhat festooned with Hungarian flags and included an occasional swastika but there was no sense that there was a war happening and the streets were lively, with people going about their everyday business. Shops were open and seemed well stocked. They moved into their elegant building and said their goodbyes to Father who set out to join his regiment after only a few days respite. Grandfather had decided not to come with them immediately and had stayed behind in Nagyvárad in a small apartment close to the centre of the city. So there were just the three of them, Mother, herself and András who was now a young teenager and would still be attending school for the next few years.

Life became hard. Father was home infrequently and, although it was wonderful to see him, it was hard to keep on saying goodbye as the war dragged on. He was not looking well and his strong Attila features were becoming shadowed and drawn. They were all losing weight as food became scarcer and less palatable. The only bright spot was the extremely infrequent distribution of Red Cross food parcels which, although in themselves welcome, held an occasional secretly inserted US dollar bill or two. These could be exchanged for a whole goose or two ducks. Hungarian currency was not too popular but US dollars were king and could buy barely remembered delights. The thing they missed most was coffee. The chicory substitute was almost undrinkable but, in any case, preferable to tea which, in Hungary, was only drunk if you were ill in bed.

Éva had had little success with her plans to study history at the University. When she attempted to enrol she was told that most of the professors had joined the armed forces and there was little to offer. She had to settle for accountancy which she did, but resignedly and without enthusiasm. Still, it would only be a stopgap until the war ended and then she could do what she wanted.

Éva had quite a long trek to the University each day. If the trams were running she was able to walk a short distance, catch a bus, then a tram over the Margit Bridge, then another tram through Pest to the University. If the trams were not running then a combination of buses was the only option. On some days she had to walk the entire distance which was not easy. Pest was quite flat but walking up the hills to her home in Sashegy was a mountainous, exhausting hike. She often did not go to University if she could not be assured of a ride home.

The war rolled on. They had their lives, their health, their home and each other. Grandfather had not ultimately come to Budapest but they knew he was safe. Whilst there was scarcity there seemed to be enough to survive on (in spite of the chicory) and they were fit from all the walking. Mami had learned to cook a few things as they were unable to keep servants but preparation of food was relatively simple in the absence of good basic Hungarian ingredients.

It all started to change in late 1944. Budapest became a target for both the Third Reich and the Russian Army. Hitler was determined that Budapest would be held and the Russians were determined that they would take it. The Red Army started to advance on Budapest.

But prior to that they had learned that Father was desperately ill.

In later life Éva wrote a letter to her cousin about her Father. This is what she wrote:

"Dear Louie

I am writing, with deep gratitude, to say a very sincere thank you to you, and all those kind people involved, who paid tribute to my late Father.

I cannot tell you how much this meant to my Mother, and my brother and myself. It is nearing three decades since my Father died. He died in agony, so that scores may live to see better days. I am sorry for never talking about this to you – but years ago my Mother and I decided that Father was so selfless, had so much courage, telling stories about him – and this coming from his own family – would only belittle the truth. Especially when we found, to our dismay, that almost every refugee had a "good story" to tell on leaving their country, so that in no time at all far too many "tall stories" – most of them obviously fabrications – were circulating around. And so, Mother and I decided that we will bury Father's memory where he was assured of everlasting love and gratitude, we will bury him deep in our hearts.

He was commanding a "yellow-armband" contingent on the Eastern Front, high in the Carpathian Mountains in the bloodstained Autumn of 1944, when we heard that he was desperately ill. Mother and I somehow managed to get to him, to plead for him to seek medical help and hospitalization. He was aghast at the suggestion! "Do you know, what will happen to these boys the day I leave"? – he asked us, - and we knew only too well! As it was, with him grimly holding on to his post, he got order after order, to pack the contingent into horse-wagons, and dispatch it to Annihilation Camps in Germany. He disobeyed the orders, all of them. As the Front approached, the orders became menacing, till he was faced with Court Martial. He still stood his ground – and the last moment he saved the ENTIRE detachment, sending them to safety over the Russian lines. He did not lose one single man! – But he lost his life. He came home desperately ill, in a city destroyed by the Siege, with no doctors, no hospital beds, no medicines. He died in agony, of cancer of the bowels, so far advanced that the doctors whom we could find in the end, marveled how he stood on his feet for the past months.

And so he left us. Bewildered and terrified, because we always lived within the shield of his greatness and love, protected from evil. – In his very few spare moments, on the front, or under bombing, he wrote verses, - and very beautiful verses they were! Each and every one of them speaks of compassion, of understanding, of love. The recurring theme in each: NEVER violate your conscience. Give up your health, your life – but NEVER your integrity! He never did, and so, today, we hope there are scores of children – the children of those "boys" he saved – who would not walk this earth, if it were not for my Father. It is very warming to our hearts to know that there are some who remember.

With love and gratitude

Éva Anna Maria Castley (nee Gyenge) [undated]"

On 2 November 1944, the Red Army approached Budapest. The bombing had been relentless and was not about to let up for the next 3 months. Budapest had been a beautiful, elegant, sophisticated city and would be reduced to filthy rubble.

The Siege of Budapest was preparing to commence.

On 4 November 1944 Éva was returning home after a shopping, scavenging expedition. The whole population of Budapest was seemingly on the move. There were overflowing buses and trams, horses and carriages even, many people walking, carrying bags and burdens of every description. Éva too was laden down with packages and containers, none of it very nourishing but all she was able to get and carry from the shops. She was on the Margit Bridge tram in the very last compartment. The tram turned onto the bridge which was immensely crowded as people and vehicles rushed to escape the advancing Russians and to get home with their small prizes. The front compartments were already lumbering onto the bridge when there was a massive explosion. Éva didn't really hear the explosion as all she felt was a shock wave and then she went quite deaf for a moment. Her hearing returned in a rush of noise and screams. The tram tilted down and seemed to be slipping gradually forward. The people in the crammed carriage were pushing and crying and shouting as the carriage rocked and slid. Then it stopped with a crunch and those people who were not already spread out and jammed confusingly every which way fell about and crashed into further odd positions. Éva had not left her seat so did not suffer the injuries which happened to those who had been ratcheted around by their own panic. She had lost all her packages and hurt her knee slightly when it had butted up against the seat in front. She was relieved to be in one piece but anxious now to leave the sloping carriage as quickly as possible. It was hard to move though as people scrambled to get to the exit doors and to get them open. One of them had sort of broken open and this was the exit which she, and most of her fellow passengers converged upon. She tried to see where her packages were but they had either slithered away to the front of the carriage or been trodden and mushed by the flailing feet of the people trying to get out as fast as possible. She finally managed to get to the split open exit door and then realized that there was further peril as the bridge itself was sloping straight down to the freezing Danube. She was glad she no longer had parcels as she carefully alighted from the tram and went on to her hands and knees so as to more safely crawl up the dangerous incline. She was also glad that she had been one of the last to get off as it was apparent some passengers had lost their footing and gone into the water. Hands began to reach out to her as she approached the top of the slab and she was dragged the last metre to safety. She was wet and dirty and seemed to be shaking. She stood up and looked at the Bridge. All tram carriages apart from hers, had sunk into the river and there was terrible screaming coming from below. A few of the passengers had managed to climb out onto the roof and were trying to make their way back to the shore along this extremely unsafe route. The whole Western side of the Bridge had gone and she thought that a lot of cars, trams and people who had been on the bridge must be in the water. She didn't have any idea what had happened but supposed it was a bomb. Later she was to learn that it had actually been an accidental bomb explosion and that over 600 people had perished.

Éva now had to make her way home on foot. It was the middle of the day and took her till much later. She thought about the Red Army and wondered if she should be frightened and maybe hurry a bit more but she was simply too exhausted to do anything other than place one foot tiredly in front of the other and eventually get home. She had nothing to show for her ordeal except a badly bruised knee and clothing which had to be thrown away.

The family had had a reasonably hard time during the war so far but the sheer degradation of the next few months was unimaginable.

Éva's brother András had been called up although he was still relatively young and this left Éva with her mother to cope with what was to come.

The Arrow Cross Party which had come to power in October would prove to be zealous administrators of the Third Reich 'final solution'. The small family had an air raid shelter which they, along with dozens of their neighbours, slept in every night. They could still hear the whines, thumps, phloom noises of the bombs in the distance.

In the mornings, after a usually sleepless night they would ascend wearily to assess the damage and commence the daily search for food.

The siege of Budapest was about to commence in earnest. It was very unfortunate that Sashegy (Eagle Hill) was one of the first strategic positions to be targeted by the opposing forces. It would be six weeks of relentless house to house fighting before the Russians could claim they had secured this key hill overlooking Buda.

The night before Christmas Eve 1944 Éva and her mother Piroska again huddled back into their shelter with the remaining neighbours. There were 32 of them. Again they sleeplessly lived through the dreadful sounds coming through to them. It seemed very close as they stared at each other in the candle lit gloom. The sounds were loud, louder than they had ever been. And then the shelter seemed to light up. Everything went white and quiet until the screaming started. The shelter had been breached by a direct hit from something and the roof had caved in on them all. Éva's foot was trapped under something and she couldn't move. She tried to move her head and was gripped by a fit of coughing which wouldn't stop as the dust from the explosion continued to fill the remnants of the shelter. She screamed for her mother who had been sitting next to her. It was impossible to see anything and it was hard to hear anything for the screaming of the others.

Then she felt a hand in hers and her mother's voice very close by said "Darling darling I'm here. Are you allright?" "Yes Mami, but I can't move my foot." "It's allright just hold my hand and we will try to breathe slowly."

They held each other's hands for a very long time. Gradually the dust settled and the screaming subsided to be replaced by sobbing and groaning. Éva held on so tightly to her mother's hand. She thought she could never let go. She could see her mother's face in the gloom at last. They were both completely covered in dust and she could taste the smashed rocks and concrete on herself as she licked her lips to get some moisture. "Mami are you hurt at all?" "No, I can move."

She looked up. There was a wrenching hole in the roof of the shelter but it was not very big and had obviously been blown through as a side effect of the bomb which had landed somewhere else on the roof and crushed the shelter on to them. She could see a few people moving slightly but the area where she was trapped with her mother was too small to move much at all. The fact that her foot was trapped was really irrelevant.

"Do you think someone will come for us – help us?" she asked her mother. "I'm sure they will soon darling."

The shelter was now very very cold as their small coal burner had been extinguished and the shelter was now open to the snow and the freezing night. Piroska shifted and moved and wriggled until her body was touching her daughter's body. "We will need to try and stay warm." There was another person very nearby who had not moved or said anything since the bomb hit them.

Her mother always carried a small emergency stash of chocolate and she broke off a small piece and pushed it through Éva's dusty lips.

It was heaven. "This is all we have to eat my darling so just a small piece now until they come and get us." "Mami I'm so thirsty." Her mother reached for a small food container and said "We will get some melted snow but it probably won't start to melt through the opening until morning. Try and sleep my darling." With her mother's warmth beside her and her acceptance of the hopelessness of the situation, Éva, surprisingly did fall into an exhausted slumber. The nearby person still did not move.

It was so cold and Éva woke to soft snow falling on her face. She licked her lips. The darkness was beginning to pale and she could see the weak light coming through the opening in the roof of the shelter. She felt despair grip her as she realized again where they were and that she couldn't move. Her trapped ankle was throbbing. She licked some more snow off her face and turned her head to look at her mother. She looked peaceful. Éva panicked. "Mami, Mami." Piroska opened her eyes. "Shhh darling I'm here." They held each other more tightly. Éva could make out some of the other people in the shelter. They were all lying in the wreck of the bomb blast, covered with grit and filth. Some were moaning and crying. Others were still and huddled. As the paleness of the light increased some woke and began screaming. "Help, help, help." More commonly the screaming was inarticulate raging which hurt your whole head to listen to.

They lay like that for hours with her mother murmuring reassuringly, sometimes just humming quietly. The food container now held some snow melt and they occasionally took small sips. Her mother was able to pass it to some others who could reach it. These small efforts exhausted them all and they slept occasionally throughout the long day.

They could all hear rifle fire, machine gun fire and explosions from nearby. Occasionally they heard voices and Éva joined with her mother and some of the others in calling for help. Their cries remained unheard or, if they were heard, unanswered. The very pale light which had greeted them on that day began to fade and the extreme cold became even colder. Mami gave Éva another small sliver of chocolate. "We can only have a small piece after it is dark," her mother whispered, "otherwise we will have to share it and there is not very much." Éva felt that her legs were now quite numb. Piroska was able to move a little but no-one was able to stand upright. Shuffling around was not productive as there were no better places to be in the shelter, but it did keep some blood flowing a little. Éva's mother wriggled to a different position where she could massage her daughter's legs. She talked to Éva and began to tell her stories from Miklósvár. She told her how she had met Éva's father at a wonderful ball where he was handsome and elegant in his officer's uniform. She told her of the joy they had in their beautiful home, how they had gone horseback riding through the woods, how they had entertained guests from as far away as Scotland and the United States. She talked and talked and Éva was able to think herself there in that magical place of safety and warmth and plenty and love, where her father was still with them and they were all happy. Again they slept a little.

The next day was a bit worse. A few more people were not moving at all and those that were lacked the energy for very much screaming. Panic had subsided, hope was being crushed, despair was taking hold. The shelter was becoming a grave site and they all felt it was just a matter of time. Her mother tried to rally those within hearing distance. Their voices were all cracked and hoarse from the lack of water but her mother tried nevertheless. "Someone will come." "They will come here." "We must take turns shouting that we are here otherwise they won't know where to dig." A roster of sorts was arranged with at least one person scheduled to shout every ten minutes or so.

From somewhere they heard singing. "It is Christmas." Her mother looked at Éva sadly. "It was Christmas Eve last night and we forgot." Éva said "Not a very happy one Mami but happy Christmas anyway." They both smiled. Then her mother said a bit more loudly. "It's Christmas everyone. Chances are that the fighting will stop and there's a better chance of us being found." With this small inspiration they began shouting all at once. "No, no, we must save our energy" her mother said. "Stick to the roster everyone."

So they lived through Christmas Day, their second day in the ruined shelter.

Christmas night came upon them. They had heard little fighting that day but no more singing after that solitary burst, the singing which had reminded them.

Éva and her mother shared some chocolate. It had never tasted so good ever in her life.

During the night they were both woken from their freezing fitful sleep by the sound of terrified screaming. "Get away, aargh, no, no, aaaah, no, get away..." "What is it?" Éva shouted. "Rats, horrible rats or something. Oh God it's horrible, go away." Everyone was awake and flailing wildly around. Éva and her mother waved their arms around. It was completely dark and the whereabouts of these slimy hungry animals was horrifyingly unknown. "No, no, we must calm down." Her mother shouted. "There is nothing we can do and we'll just exhaust ourselves. There probably are rats but they will only be interested in the dead bodies. We might feel and hear them but they won't hurt us. We just have to put up with it." Another awful thing to put up with, Éva thought. She felt an overwhelmingly rush of love for her mother. How brave and steady she was. Where did it come from, this strength? She wondered if she would become strong like her mother one day. Then she thought that there may not be a one day. Maybe they would be found but it was already too late for some of them. Would they all be dead when they were found? There were so many dead in Budapest, a few more wouldn't make much difference.

Her mother's words had settled people somewhat although there were still small shouts of disgust every now and then. No rats had come near Éva and her mother but there did not seem to be any dead people particularly close to them so they might be spared.

They were all filthy. Éva's mouth, apart from being dry and cracked, was horrible tasting and foul. The clothes they were wearing when they came into the shelter were not that clean to start with and they were now matted with dust. By the fourth day the itching began. Éva tried to scratch but it was never enough. She noticed small red marks on her mother's face. There was very little of their skin which was exposed and she supposed she had bites or marks on her as well. So itchy. She scratched and scratched at her head. Her mother said "We must have insects biting us." Éva knew better. She knew that it was lice. She had seen it before on other people. She had always thought that they would not get lice because they had at least tried to wash themselves as best they could and wear reasonably clean clothing. That was now a thing of the past. Thankfully because they had so little to drink and no food at all to speak of, they had been forced to soil themselves only minimally. And not at all after the first 36 hours in the shelter. Even so, Éva felt completely disgusting and beyond dirty to the point where she hated her body. She could scratch herself to death for all she cared, even though her mother tried to stop her from time to time.

By the fifth day in the shelter there were many more dead. Éva wished by now that she also was dead. She was weak and dizzy when she was awake, but her dehydrated and starved body forced her to sleep most of the time. She wondered when she might not wake up again.

Her mother continued to speak to her gently of their lost paradise in Transylvania and all the glories that would await them when they returned.

The nights became much much harder to bear as the rat population increased. They could hear them slithering and snuffling about and, worse, they could hear the soft guzzling and squeaking slurping sounds they made as they feasted on their friends and neighbours. It was almost intolerable. The days were better as the rats seemed to prefer the nights. This was mostly when they were able to sleep. Her mother began to talk to her of a fantastic fabulous dress. "When we are rescued from here, I will make you the finest, most beautiful Hungarian gala dress that has ever been seen," she promised her daughter. She described in every detail how it would rival the court regalia of the Queens of Hungary, how it would be covered with thousands of semi-precious stones and be made of the most wonderful velvet which could be had. She promised Éva she would do this because her daughter was beautiful and would be seen in all the best places with the best people. She would wear it at a very special ball in Miklósvár to welcome the family home again.

They talked of this for hours, with Éva demanding more and more detail so she could imagine herself somewhere else, looking splendid.

Their sordid existence had fallen into a sort of pattern. The nights were spent staying reasonably alert for rat incursions, scratching at the nasty bites which by now were all over them, conversations about better and more wondrous times, details of the gala dress which would be made by Éva's mother, trying to move as much as possible to keep circulation in their legs and to keep the rats away and the occasional sleep. They did not do much scheduled shouting for help during the night as there seemed little point. The snow had obviously continued falling and falling (which at least ensured their supply of drinking water) and there seemed to be only minimal fighting happening in the blizzardy darkness. The daytime was for sleeping mainly, although the scheduled shouting interrupted this somewhat. It was for gathering and melting snow and for counting the dead. Her mother continued to try and keep those still alive hopeful but it was becoming very much harder.

They tried to keep a tally of the days and by their reckoning it was eight days since they had been buried in this unforgiving bomb site. It was New Year's Eve. The light in the shelter seemed brighter that morning as they rubbed and scratched themselves into a sort of awakeness. There were very few of them left. The smell which had started about three or four days earlier was intolerable, sickly and revolting. Most of the rotting bodies had been gnawed and disfigured by the rats who had now become greater in number as the offerings increased. Those remaining, including Éva and her mother, were so weak that even the effort of sipping a little water or moving any limb slightly was almost too much.

The brightness increased in the shelter and a pile of rubble fell in on them.

"My God there are people alive in here." They heard someone shouting above them and a face peered in then disappeared. They heard some excited movements above them. "Be careful, we don't want to bring the whole thing down on them." More rubble fell in then, after the opening had been made to a width of about a metre, a ladder was pushed in and down to them. A Russian soldier came down the ladder, gazed around him with horror and then added to the filth and decay, by throwing up the contents of his stomach.

The soldiers pulled the small number of those still alive up and out of the shelter one by one. Each one was able to be pulled up by just a single soldier. Lying on the fresh snow in the sunlight out of that monstrous tomb was so pleasurable, no-one wanted to move. The Russians shouted at them in Russian "You must run, there are snipers and it is not safe." The Hungarians were not able to understand what was being said but the urgency of the gestures and the rifle barrels poked into them were translation enough to get them on their feet. As were the bullets which started zinging past them from nearby buildings.

Éva got to her feet. She really didn't know how she could stand. Her ankle was twisted and obviously broken, she was starved to the point of near death and she had not really moved at all for eight days. However she ran across that snow until she reached a building and then collapsed with pain against the wall. Her mother had been running with her but was no longer there. She saw that Piroska had run back through the sniper fire to the Russian soldiers, then was turning and running back towards her again. Éva watched in desperation as her mother, alone, ran and stumbled to safety. "Mami" she screamed "why did you go back?" Her mother fell down beside her. "I dropped the chocolate and had to go back to find it." She gasped. Icy tears were slowly freezing into the caked dirt on their faces. Again they clung together sobbing. It was the eve of Éva's 25th birthday.

Many decades later Éva wrote what happened next.

"WAR 1945

[I was half way across the snow-covered paddock when the sun came out from between two dark clouds and the sudden brightness nearly blinded me. I turned to recover my sight – and] this section crossed out

I trudged half way across the snow covered paddock when a stray winter sun-ray in my eyes forced me to turn. Blurring and dazed I surveyed my erring footsteps zig-zagging across the icing-sugar snow. I felt dizzy and weightless and drunkenly I leant against a stump. I contemplated for a moment sitting down – but then there were too many crouching figures sitting or lying in the snow, and I idly wondered whether they felt light-headed like me before they gave it up. The scene truly fitted the day, New Years day – the drunken foot-steps, the crouching figures – perhaps a familiar sight after a particularly gay Silvester night. But there was a difference today, the crouching figures were dead – the date was 1st Jan 1945. The only gay thing about last night was the fact that a Russian platoon after the germans, in hideouts, dug us out from under the rubble of a two-storey building after 8 days being trapped without food and water. When the fatal bomb came there were 32 of us in the shelter under the house. When the first soldier reached us last night there were 8 left. Not much left of us either – for the soldier hardened in 6 years of battles, leant against the wall and was sick on the floor at the sight of us. Shockingly mutilated bodies, corpses everywhere – and 8 living skeletons. I have a hazy recollection of the next few hours – the rat-tat of machine-gun fire as we were told to get out and run for the shelter of the next house where a Russian command was. How all of us fell down and licked the snow with tongues swollen and blackened out of all proportion – oblivious to the shooting going on – how we were told we had to get out and walk [after several drinks of...warm...,...] several miles across a hill to get to the village beyond, out of the military zone. And we started – and got there, six of us. Two more died on the road. And now I was sent out to get food – to beg for food, for I was the youngest, I was [....] And it was my birthday today. Wearily I started again and commenced begging at the first ruin that seemed to shelter life. But the inhabitants were like me – emaciated, frightened, stripped of almost every human attribute. They simply pushed me out. At one place a kindly old woman told me there was a Russian field-kitchen at the end of the road in the only still standing house, and some of the cooks speak a little German. I went. Right in. The sight must have shocked them; a tall skeleton of a girl with long pigtails, 5ft.6inches weighing a little over 5 stone. The shock kept them speechless for a moment and I got my story in, in halting German, about the six of us in the coal-cellar down the road, with old women and an 11 year old child with us, no food. Please, in name of God, just some bones. An elderly man with a graying moustache broke their shock. All right, all right – he said in German, I suppose to stop my hysterical story, and started towards the table with a half-pork laid out on it. His words broke their spell. Nearest to me stood a young officer. He went red with fury and hatred. Simply picked me up by my pigtails and with a well aimed kick sent me sailing down the 5 or 6 steps of the kitchen to finish flat on my face. I can't say it hurt. I was long past the stage where anything or anybody could hurt me. A sort of numbness returned over my brains – and I trudged back towards the coal-cellar followed by their coarse laughter.

It was cold and sinister in the cellar – someone got a small stove from the ruins above and with the coal it kept the place warm, gave a light of some sort. Everyone was lying on various rags or pieces of furniture scavenged from the ruins around. Another of the old ladies has gone – a tired voice told me. Any food? No. I can't say I even cared any more. I sat down next to Mother and held her hand – the hand that brought me up, that kept me alive 8 dreary days and nights while I was trapped under the *falling beams, the hand that guided me across minefields last night stepping ahead of me. Mother who was always there who was as much a necessity to my life as God Himself. Her hands were cold. Are you cold? I whispered. No, she said, just tired and weak. And then in whisper: I don't think I'll live till tomorrow. The words struck me the most terrible shock of my life. Mother, gentle, spoilt Mother, who rose to heights of unparalleled heroism during the months of horror and siege to save life to save those she loved. – Mother is going. For lack of food. For me failing to get a piece of that pork, for the Russian being stronger than me. I do hope none of us will ever be called again to go to the end of human endurance – then asked to go on. Somehow I did. The numbness and dizziness went – all that was left was a fury a towering rage against life in general and the Russian in particular who refused me the meat. I never faltered on the way back. I cannot say when I first thought about murder. But I chose a corpse (there were many scattered about) with a gun with a bayonet and carefully removed the bayonet. I remember wiping the dried, frozen blood off it. Then proceeded back to the Russian field-kitchen. Going around the back I tried to climb in through a window, and was half in when a Russian came into the back room. Mercifully it was the old, German speaking kitchen-hand soldier. I am sure if it were the younger soldier he would have simply shot me. The old soldier just saw a young emaciated girl, with bayonet raised, and he hit it out of my hand. He lifted me into the room, and soon returned with a horse-bucket full with steaming soup. He helped me back to the coal-cellar and kept us alive for days with food. He explained that back in Russia he had a girl just my age, with pigtails, and he was hoping someone is keeping her alive in this terrible war. We prayed for this girl every night and the Russian soldier joined us when he brought along our daily bucket of soup. He showed us a crucifix on a string on his neck and said if his superiors would know about it, he could be shot."*

When the bombings began to intensify during the siege dead bodies became commonplace but Éva saw many corpses which had clearly not died from bombing raids. Throats had been cut or heads had been blown away by carefully aimed bullets. Éva had some Jewish friends, one of whom was living with them. She asked to borrow Éva's identification papers if she needed to go out. This was frightening because they would both be shot if she was discovered. But everyone was frightened of everything and Éva was living in a dazed, half starved state most of the time so this fear was just one more.

The Red Cross food parcels were a thing of the past and food became very hard to find.

Scavenging was a daily occupation and so was looting. Anyone with a gun was reasonably well fed as they could take what little there was to have. Éva walked incessantly, entering houses which had been bombed in the hope of finding some tins or jars which could help sustain them. Mostly she resigned herself to finding dead bodies.

Very few of the dead were removed. There was no-one to bury them and they were left to rot. The rats which were attracted to this harvest were not initially considered edible but this changed as the Siege intensified.

And it was so very cold. The snow had started early. At least they had lots of warm clothes. And plenty more were available from the ruined houses.

The aerial bombings were not to be the worst of it. The Russian troops and their allies were now fighting against the German and

Hungarian troops street to street, house to house. Machine gun emplacements and mortar launchers were everywhere and days were no longer safer than nights.

There were many days Éva would never forget. They seared into her brain and continued to flash terrible terrible images all her life. There was, unfortunately, a large selection, each one worse than the next. She was out one evening scavenging with her mother and they were both treading carefully through the debris of broken glass, the fallen rubble of buildings and the bodies which lay scattered, many of them soldiers but quite a few civilians, including children and old people who had fallen victim to building collapse, rifle or machine gun fire, anti tank weapons or maybe just starvation. They didn't usually venture out in the evenings but had failed to find anything to eat earlier in the day so were hoping for some luck. Éva was slightly ahead of her mother and, as she rounded the corner of a half standing building she ran straight into a group of four of five Russian soldiers all of whom seemed cheerfully drunk. She stopped in her tracks and tried to press herself into the twilight darkness of the building but they saw her. Two of them lurched towards her while the others began to shout and laugh. She screamed for her mother who was yet to appear. By the time her mother ran around the corner and took in what was happening, Éva was well surrounded by the staggering soldiers. Her mother's face was dead white and she shouted at the soldiers. They took no notice as they now started to try and drag Éva into the building. Her mother ripped off her coat, pulled up her skirt and waved her arms in the air at the soldiers. "Take me, take me" she shouted and lewdly gestured at them. This caught their attention and the ones holding Éva let go as they turned towards the spectacle of an emaciated but attractive 50 year old woman seemingly offering herself to them. She screamed at her daughter "Run, run, run, run." Éva was sobbing and shaking and frozen to the spot. Her mother shouted again "You must run now. I love you and for love you must RUN NOW." Éva stumbled and moved. The soldiers were now fully engaged with her mother's charades and were really so drunk that they failed to care that Éva was slipping away. Éva left her mother there and ran, slipping and stumbling and sobbing, back to her home. When she got there she got into bed and cried as if she would never stop until her mother returned some hours later. Éva heard her in the house and called out to her. "Mami Mami, Mami." "Just a minute darling, I need to wash my face." A little later her mother came into her bedroom and wordlessly crept into bed beside Éva where they huddled together until they slept.

One morning after they had wrapped themselves well in their coats and scarves and climbed from the cellar they saw that their house had suffered a direct hit from either an aerial or a land based attack. But it was not all that bad. The dining room had exploded but most of the other rooms were intact and they were able to continue to live there. There was no electricity and no running water. Neither of these was a particular problem as there was nothing to cook and they were able to melt snow over candles for drinking. Many of their dining room ornaments had ended up in the snow outside. These were of little interest to looters whose main preoccupation was food and also alcohol.

A young woman who had failed to find shelter for the night was lying in the icy street. Half her head had been destroyed but, although fully clothed to her waist, the rest of her was naked. Éva and her mother absorbed this grim fact and recognized that the rapacious nature of the invading Soviets was without human decency. Whether she had been raped while still alive or not was unknown.

It was late January and they had started to eat horse meat which was by now the only available food apart from their tiny stockpile of a few tins and jars and some more chocolate which they had carefully hidden and, of course, the wonderful mouthfuls of Russian soup. Horse meat was not that easy to come by as any dead horse was almost instantly surrounded by people anxious to cut as much as they could and get away with it. You had to be in the right place at the right time. Éva pondered sometimes on what it was to be lucky and how the standard had changed beyond recognition.

They tried to keep clean but it was very difficult.

Budapest had been reduced to rubble. There were few houses left standing. The streets were blocked with fallen masonry, broken glass, barbed wire, dead bodies, mortar shells and other armament discards and rubbish.

The sheer misery of it all was almost beyond bearing. Éva and Piroska lived from hour to hour, minute to minute. The small quantities of soup provided by the old Russian soldier kept them barely alive. They were warm as wood and coal remained reasonably plentiful. They were reduced to living like scavenging animals. They rarely ventured out. It was miserable and dangerous. The fighting was everywhere, all around them and a bullet or a mine could end their precarious lives at any minute. The Arrow Cross members became ever more arrogant, bursting in at all hours, rounding up Jews or young men, even young women who could be conscripted into fighting units. The Russian soldiers continued to hold the Hungarians in some contempt and sometimes they were the first to loot valuables or any stores of food or alcohol. The rapes continued and were to become more frequent as the siege neared its end and moved to the next dreary and repellant stage of Russian occupation and dominance.

On 13 February Budapest surrendered to the Soviet Army and its allies, including the Romanians. Before the War it had been a city of about one million people.

The toll on this once beautiful and elegant city during the 102 days of the Siege was: 75% of all buildings damaged, 80,000 dead Russian and allied soldiers, 240,000 wounded Russian and allied soldiers, 40,000 dead German and allied soldiers, 60,000 wounded German and allied soldiers, 100,000 Jews deported or murdered, 40,000 dead civilians and up to 200,000 civilian rapes.

Life continued to be terribly difficult. Éva and Piroska sometimes spoke of the fact that the actual siege had been perhaps preferable to the daily miseries of Soviet military rule. At least the shelling, fighting, shooting and bombing had stopped. But the sheer adrenaline of the combat had helped them survive intolerable hardships. Now they were reduced to ongoing degrading daily misery in a ruined city. They had little hope for the future. Lajos Gyenge came home from the Eastern front and was welcomed with joy. His excruciatingly lingering painful death over the next few months gave them a renewed focus with at least short term hope to relieve them. Will he live through this day, the next day, the next day. Will he look a little better today. Will he take some nourishment. Will he smile or speak. Will his pain be a little less. He died and was taken to the nearest hospital. There was no funeral and the final resting place of his body was never to be known.

The Red Cross provided some food and medical assistance. This included tins of DDT powder to help rid the city of its chronic lice infestation. Typhus was the fear but the immediate relief to be had from the bites, the itching and the disgusting effect the lice had on human morale was not to be under estimated. Éva and Piroska gaily dowsed themselves in this toxic substance and felt a small jolt of happiness that this filthy thing at least would be gone from their lives.

They continued to live in their half ruined house on Sashegy. The Red Army soldiers were everywhere. There were some attempts to clean the streets, at least rid the city of the dead and rotting corpses of soldiers and civilians. Life continued at a miserable, reduced pace.

Some food was available but only if you had money or valuables to pay for it.

In a few months the War would be over bringing joy to many but not to those who were now occupied by a foreign power. The Russians held to their grip on Hungary although it was not until 1949 that they did this forcibly after some failed token elections where the Communist candidates were resoundingly defeated.

Éva and Piroska moved to a flat in Pest. András joined them. They made plans. They had quite substantial assets most of which were still available to them. Thankfully not much was in cash as devastating inflation had reduced the value of any Hungarian cash to less than worthless. Piroska had some contacts in the Red Cross and, given their bleak future in Hungary, they decided that, if possible, Éva should emigrate to another country and then organize for the rest of the family to follow. This could be done simply via an arranged marriage with someone who was already a citizen of that country. They discussed the options and decided that the countries which seemed keenest on European immigrants were Canada and Australia. There would be likely to be less scrutiny of any hurried or odd looking marriage arrangements.

In 1948 Éva travelled to Paris and boarded a BOAC flying boat for the long trip to Australia.

4. Tasmania

Éva had lost her first home, had left her second home, been bombed out of her third home and fretfully left her mother and brother in her fourth home to travel alone across the world to marry a man she had never met. She was 28 and had lost her entire country, first by annexation and then by occupation. Her courage and grief was all she had left.

The marriage was a disaster and ended very quickly by mutual agreement. Éva worked at odd jobs and enrolled at the University in Geography. She made friends, lots of them. Some were attracted to the exotic nature of this Transylvanian immigrant but even these became firm and genuine friends after the novelty wore off and they understood what a rare human being they had encountered. A few of these friends knew or were related to people in high places and favours were called in to try and expedite Piroska's travel to Australia. Éva's brother had married but he was not to escape from Hungary until much later, well after the failed 1956 'revolution'. In spite of the favours and the friends it was to be three long years before Piroska finally arrived on the 'Caboto' in 1951.

Éva and Piroska set up house together, first in a small leaky cottage in Montagu Bay which was destined to be the exact spot where a Tasman Bridge pylon would find its home. Éva had saved money from her small salaries and she still had funds which she had brought with her so they built a house in Darling Parade which was to be their home for the next few years. Éva now had a job as an accountant. Not officially of course as her qualifications were not recognized. Her skills were obvious and she did not have any problem finding jobs, albeit at a wage which reflected somewhat the exploitative nature of such arrangements.

She was ultimately employed by Charles Castley who operated a successful small loans business in Cat and Fiddle Arcade. Charles was married with two children. Indeed, Charles already had another two children by a previous marriage. He was also 20 years older than Éva.

Charles fell flat on his face with love. He divorced his second wife and married Éva in 1959. The house in Darling Parade was sold and the three of them moved to Sydney. Charles owned the Cornwall Hotel in Launceston which he had bought during the depression. This was leased in order to gain a steady income.

Éva's brother, wife and two small children had escaped from Hungary and they joined them.

It seemed as though Éva could now look forward to happiness and peace with her brother, her mother and her husband.

The Cornwall Hotel was leased to an ex-Richmond football player called Jeff Patterson. He seemed a nice enough chap, back slapped and drank with everyone in the bar. He also went to the horse races and, although the hotel was doing very well, he steadily, gradually and inexorably drained it of funds to feed his gambling habit. Not only drained but borrowed, ran up debts and left his accounts unpaid.

Creditors contacted Charles and begged him to return, which he did, hoping it could be a quick fix. But the damage was too great, in the order of $250,000 which for the 1950s, was an enormous amount of money. Patterson left the country. In later years he was to return to glowing reports in the local newspaper stating that he had repaid every debt and was a changed man. He did not contact Charles and Charles was never to be repaid anything. But Patterson was a popular con man and the truth was a casualty.

So, after a short period of happiness the small family returned to Launceston. Éva's brother Andrew and his family stayed in Sydney so it was just the three of them.

Charles was nearing sixty years of age but proceeded to work 24 hours a day. Éva's accountancy skills were put to good use. Additionally she, along with Charles, waited on tables, acted as receptionist, haggled with banks, hired and fired staff, dealt with drunks, served behind the bar, and did all the range of neverending jobs and tasks required of hotel keepers. Most of their earnings went straight to the creditors and banks. Piroska lived in a flat in Elphin Rd where Charles and Éva could go from time to time for a meal or even a decent sleep. Most of the time they lived their lives in Room 109 at the top of the stairs on the first floor so that they could quickly get downstairs to let someone in.

Éva became pregnant. She was forty. She miscarried the first time, then the second time, then the third time, then the fourth time. Her fifth pregnancy in 1961 was full term and a baby girl was born on 22 October after five days in labour. She was Marie-Charlotte and she lived for just two days. Éva and Charles and Piroska were consumed with grief. Éva blamed Launceston, the stress, the workload and what she believed to be incompetent obstetricians.

No more pregnancies were attempted. The death of a baby is just too hard and she was now nearing forty two.

Grief for Marie-Charlotte was tucked away, allowed to surface only on those rare quiet occasions when Éva could be alone and sobbing into 'The Trojan Women'.

They worked and worked and worked. Moderate happiness was re-achieved. Another trauma had been dealt with and she had survived but she felt a pit of longing and love which ate at her.

PART TWO: SHIRLEY

5. Balikpapan, Hobart and Launceston

1945: Borneo

The Australian soldiers were weary. Most of them had joined up at the start of the War and it was hard to believe that they had been sent overseas again just as everyone was starting to say the War was nearly over. But here they were in Balikpapan doing heaven knows what to stop something which probably wouldn't happen anyway.

Cyril Gibbons, known as Johnny to his mates, was particularly weary. He had seen the world mostly through a machine gun sight. He had been sent overseas four times, the first to the Middle East when he was 16 years old. The Army didn't know he was 16 and didn't much care either. He and his father had joined up together. Like many others it was the excitement which had drawn them. It certainly seemed to promise greater interest than a life of tin mining in Derby in North West Tasmania, a town of just some hundreds.

In 1943 on one of his trips back to Australia, he had married and had a son.

He had thought being in Crete was the very worst time of his life. Lots of his mates had been killed or wounded in front of his eyes. He had gone AWOL a few times probably in the faint hope he would be sent back home. However, despite time spent in a military prison in Australia for being again AWOL and drunk and disorderly, the Army had just kept on sending him into battle. This last time in Borneo had been the final straw. It was worse than Crete. He was so very tired of it all and here he was again. It was hot and sticky and now it seemed they were fighting off the Japanese. The Germans, the Japanese, what difference did it make? It was all the same. He was either too hot or too cold, his clothes were never clean, the food was monotonous and insufficient, there was never enough sleep to be had, the sounds of shells, planes, machine guns were all the same. He missed his wife and son, he missed feeling safe.

His head hurt and he needed a drink. In some places the troops had been able to get away to small local bars to drink and sing and stagger back to wherever they were stationed. Not here though. It really was too hot and their uniforms, such as they were, were bedraggled and minimal. Most of the soldiers were stripped down to a pair of misshapen shorts and boots. That meant they were prey to any insects and there were plenty of those.

He endured.

After the official end of the War he finally came home and was discharged at last. He had spent most of his teenage years at war and had little or nothing to show for it except bad dreams and a lost youth.

The visceral unnamed need which had been bred by the continual fight, flight adrenaline routine of War led him to join the Police Force. Many felt the same need and the Police Force of 1946 in Australia seemed filled with young weary Constables who lived for the small quivers and shudders of violence which they had so longed to escape but which now seemed as necessary as breathing to keep them feeling alive.

In October 1946 I was born, a younger sister to my brother. Apparently a sickly child, nearly dead of pneumonia as a baby, kept alive by my father feeding me with an eye dropper day and night.

I do not know if it was ever a happy marriage. It is impossible to judge such things. Johnny drank, a lot. Mostly with his police mates. It was the culture and he fitted in.

Do women and men react differently to the fear and horror of War? Éva felt some of the same attraction to violence and disaster as Johnny did but what she felt was empathy. He felt super charged. She felt super sorrow.

MERCURY newspaper: Thursday 13 October 1949

"HOBART CONSTABLE PLEADS NOT GUILTY TO CHARGES OF "MANHANDLING"

Constable Cyril Edward Gibbons of Hobart pleaded not guilty in the Hobart Police Court to a charge of having on July 22nd last used unnecessary violence to a prisoner in lawful custody.

The charge was laid under Police Regulations and Superintendent Dowling is prosecuting.

Gibbons is represented by Mr W.C.Hodgman.

After hearing evidence yesterday Mr G.F.Sorell PM adjourned the case until October 20th.

The charge is a sequel to complaints of manhandling made in the Hobart Police Court recently by Royden James Grubb, tally clerk, of Moonah, who was convicted of being drunk and disorderly.

In Court yesterday, Grubb said that on the night of July 22 the manager of the Imperial Hotel, Hobart, called the police to remove him from the hotel on the grounds that he was making a nuisance of him-self.

"Pushed To Pavement"

Grubb said he had admitted being "merry," but not drunk.

Grubb said Gibbons entered the hotel and ordered him to leave.

"When I was going out the door, Gibbons pushed me out on to the pavement and then struck me on the base of the skull," said Grubb.

"I lay in the gutter in a dazed condition."

Gibbons dragged him to his feet by the throat and ear, punched him on the mouth, and knocked him down again, Grubb said.

He was taken to the police station in a motor cycle and side-car.

Outside the charge-room, Grubb alleged, Gibbons struck him on the head, face, and chest, as a result of which he lost consciousness.

At 11.30 p.m. Gibbons further assaulted him in the lock-up, while a sergeant stood in the doorway, Grubb stated.

Next morning he was charged with being drunk and disorderly, and was released on bail.

Grubb admitted being convicted on the charge later.

He said he did not seek medical attention until six days after the alleged assault, because his wife had been caring for him.
When he was troubled with a pain in the base of the skull, he went to a doctor.

"Very Drunk"

Walter Richard Fairweather, manager of the Imperial Hotel, said he ordered Grubb off the premises be I cause of complaints that he had been annoying two receptionists.

"Grubb was very drunk," Fairweather said.

When Grubb refused to leave the hotel, Fairweather phoned the police.
Fairweather said at no time did he see Gibbons assault Grubb.

"When Gibbons was assisting him through the door, I heard Grubb asking him to remove his coat and 'have a go,' " he added.

Phillip Leonard Bugg, trooper, of Tarraleah, said he was with Gibbons when Grubb was ordered out of the hotel. ,

Beyond a "reasonably mild" push, Gibbons did not assault Grubb, he added.

Mr. Hodgman intimated he had about eight witnesses to call in defence of Gibbons.

THE MERCURY: Tuesday 25th October 1949

HOBART CONSTABLE CLEARED
OF UNNECESSARY VIOLENCE CHARGE

MR. G; F. SORELL, P.M., dismissed a charge against a Hobart police constable of having used unnecessary violence to a prisoner in lawful custody when the case concluded in the Hobart Police Court yesterday.

CONSTABLE Cyril Edward .Gibbons pleaded not guilty to the charge, which was laid under Police Regulations.

Gibbons was represented by Mr. W Hodgman. Insp. G. M. Smith prosecuted.

Air. M. G. Everett appeared for Royden James Grubb.

Gibbons was alleged to have used unnecessary violence to Royden James Grubb, a tally clerk, of Moonah, when he arrested Grubb on July 28.

The complaints were made when Grubb was convicted in the Hobart Police Court of having been drunk and disorderly.
"Assaulted In Cells"

In a previous hearing, Grubb alleged that Gibbons knocked him down outside the Imperial Hotel after he had been removed from the premises at the request of the manager.

Grubb also said Gibbons knocked him into unconsciousness outside the Police Charge Room and assaulted him in the cells.

In his defence, Gibbons said at the hearing on Thursday that Grubb "kneed" him while being searched. After a second assault of this nature, he slapped Grubb across the mouth.

Yesterday, Gibbons said he struck Grubb to avoid injury to himself. The injuries for which Grubb had been treated by a doctor could not have been caused by the slap he gave Grubb.

He said Grubb had his glasses on all the time and they were not broken.

The force he used was no more than was necessary to restrain Grubb.

To Mr. Hodgman, Gibbons said the slap he gave Grubb was not hard. He did not see any blood.

"Most Disquieting"

Mr. Sorell said charges of such a nature were most disquieting to the public and could go a long way towards affecting the reputation of the Police Force.

A constable was entitled to use reasonable force in restraining a prisoner. Constables should not allow themselves to be "hacked" about. However, a constable was not entitled to handle a man roughly.

Police constables had a difficult job, and they, often had to act instinctively. This should be considered.

"However, citizens have certain rights, and if the rights of people are infringed -it is a bad thing for the country," he said.

Mr. Sorell said Grubb, on his own admission, had been drinking most of the afternoon. Witnesses said he was very drunk. "

There was no corroboration of Grubb's allegations that he was hurled through the door of the hotel and struck down,
"Action Justified"

"I can find nothing to prove that Grubb was brutally bashed outside the hotel," Mr. Sorell added.

The Magistrate said he could find nothing to sustain Grubb's charges that he was brutally assaulted at the Charge Room.

Neither the sergeant nor constable at the Charge Room saw or heard anything of a brutal assault.

Gibbons' action in slapping Grubb was justified.

"I don't recommend it or suggest that it should be done, but the constable was entitled to protect his own body," he added.

He could find nothing to prove that Gibbons had assaulted Grubb in the cells.

Decision on costs was reserved."

[Articles courtesy of the Mercury]

SELECTIVE FAMILY TREE:

Ray – Shirley – Graham – Sandra – Leanne

Cyril Edward Gibbons (f) Florence Violet Mary Wallis (m)

Cyril Edward Alfred Gibbons (f) b.1900 m. Florence May Taggart (m) 1921

George Edward Gibbins (f) b.1870 m. Mary Teresa Beatrice Leslie (m)

Edward Gibbins CONVICT transported for counterfeiting. (f) b.1816 m. Mary Elizabeth Grosvenor (m) b.1845 m. 1864

Mary's parents: William Grosvenor CONVICT b.1797 m. Elizabeth Ann Watkins b.1815

Two convicts turned up in record time. Great great grandfather and great great great grandfather. Decision made not to scratch for any more details.

More children followed. A son in 1949, another daughter in 1952 and then, in 1961 another daughter. The dreariness of their existence was lit up by this late addition. She was a joy for the whole family, sweet and funny and just a darling to have around. Johnny doted on her and took her with him whenever he could. He could relate to tiny children but not to his eldest. Ray (first born) and I were a mystery to him and he was a mystery to us.

Ray excelled at school. I excelled right up until I went to High School. I was too young.

My childhood was a dark pit of unhappiness. Many stories have been told of childhoods just such as this and not all of them Irish. Ray was a withdrawn, shy, highly intelligent boy. I was probably the same although not a boy. I often wished I were a boy although they didn't seem to have it all that much better.

We moved to Launceston when I was about five or six and, although I have some blurry memories of the place we moved from, Deloraine, my childhood was largely spent in the half renovated weatherboard house in East Launceston. My father had decided to rebuild the front verandah but apart from a feeble attempt at demolition this never eventuated and we lived with a strange, half demolished front verandah for all of my childhood.

My father's presence in the house was overwhelming. The room he occupied was never the one we wanted to be in. Thankfully his job as a policeman, later detective, kept him out of the house for a fair amount of time.

I have searched for happy memories to provide some sort of counter balance to the void of our lives but they are few and far between.

I first fell in love with a woman when I was on a bus, aged eight. It wasn't the last time. I distinctly recall being frustrated at the thought that I was definitely too young for her to even notice me let alone fall in love back.

Conversation with my father was exceptionally minimal. It involved being told to do something or, more frequently, not to do something. He had to be approached for special permissions. These usually involved money for something – an activity which could not be paid for out of our pocket money, or activities at hours where we could be expected to be not doing such things. I was slightly addicted to a radio program which was scheduled at an hour past my usual bedtime. My father would usually grunt permission for this, unless there had been some kind of behavioural transgression. In these instances I wouldn't even bother asking for permission.

When I was about fifteen we took a trip to the mainland to 'visit relatives'. To this day I have no idea who these relatives might have been. A vague notion of Aunties comes to mind. The trip involved packing us all into the latest car (always a Holden and replaced every year) and travelling by boat to Melbourne. The baby was with us so there were two adults in the front seat, plus a baby, and four of us in the back seat. Not comfortable. The trip from Melbourne to Sydney was punctuated by frequent stops on the side of the road so that the baby could be fed. We escaped from the car for a brief period of time into the blazing sun and a blanket of flies. We stopped at a motel on the way and shared the one room. My father was a terrible snorer possibly due to his beer drinking habits. The room itself is remembered as being completely covered in brown shag pile, including the walls but maybe it was just generally a horrible place. When we arrived in Sydney we stayed at the

Peoples' Palace which was my first experience of staying in a high rise hotel, which I rather took to. We ran riot throughout that very basic, Salvation Army accommodation. I very nearly killed my little brother when I dared him to try and fit into the bottom drawer of the wardrobe. The wardrobe took this indignity for a while and then toppled over, crashing onto the iron bedstead and smashing the mirrored front all over the room. Thankfully my little brother was unhurt although that might be a positive spin. I gashed my finger helping him out of the drawer and we bled our way all down the corridor, into the lift and down to Reception to get some help. My father wasn't around and I think I may have been lucky on this occasion as the hotel never told them about it.

The return journey back to Melbourne must have found us short of cash as we did not book into a motel, with or without shag pile.

Rather we "slept" in the car just outside Gundagai which was a nasty experience and one which nearly killed us all. On "waking" in the morning, and after we had weed in the bushes my father started the car and headed off at a tidy speed over the bridge. He was probably not properly awake and lost control, putting the car into a skid which left us all in a heap in the back seat and the car straddled across the middle of the bridge. No damage done to car or people but there was little conversation for the next long stretch to Melbourne. There was little conversation at the best of times.

My little brother Graham and I were a gang. I was the boss.

Our adventures were minimal but usually ended in some form of disaster. Many of them focused on the house next door which belonged to the Anglican Minister and his family. The house also came with a church.

The adventures often came with a 4 am start. I would instruct Graham to be in my room at 4 am and then I would tell him what to do. I have no idea how he knew it was 4 am. My instruction was based on the fact that I had no idea when it would be 4 am so he had better. I assume he sat upright in his bed until a suitable amount of darkness had passed and then creep to my room. This bedroom was blessed with access to the front door and a large window. As it was an adventure we naturally left by the window. Early mishaps included doing wheelies in the church car park on our bikes which were strictly forbidden during daylight hours. In the morning when gravel rash and bleeding knees were noted by our mother she would sigh and clean us up and whisper "Don't let your father see".

One notable evening or early morning I decided that we should climb up on to the church hall roof and remove as many slates as possible so that the hall would leak and no more Sunday School could be held until it was fixed. This was a good plan until we found that the slates were extremely heavy and difficult to remove so we only managed about four or five. For some reason totally unknown we were caught out. It is highly probable that we were the only suspects. One welcome punishment on this occasion was for me to be banned from Brownies and to be forbidden to become a Girl Guide. Hallelujah. Graham was not usually punished as he was clearly an 'other rank'.

I had joined the church choir. Not because I could sing but because the choir had easy access to the vestry which held a full size billiard table. I became very proficient at both playing and scoring but never did learn how to sing.

School was perfectly allright and seemed terribly easy. I came top in Grade 6 and remember much discussion about whether I was too young for High School. There was a technicality which is mystifying. Apparently if I didn't go to High School no-one else could because I had come top. So I went.

These are my happy memories. A fairly mixed bag really.

I think I was an insolent child. It was one way of dealing with the world.

My father would punish us in the manner of the day, with a heavy belt which was wielded with some vigour. All infractions were punished so we tried to avoid being caught which led to a secretiveness which was vaguely unhealthy. I caught the lion's share of it as I was always in trouble. Ray was studious and perhaps unadventurous. He kept his head down. Graham was sometimes punished but not if I was involved in the mischief which I usually was. Sandra was a lot younger but would have developed as a miscreant if she had the chance. I was beaten for wagging school which I did frequently even in Primary School. I was beaten for stealing chocolate from the local shop, AND made to go back and apologise, which I thought was over the top. I was beaten for ripping up Ray's encyclopaedias. I was beaten for making Graham jump off the woodshed roof. I jumped off too as it was just the right height for not hurting yourself too much. I was beaten for not doing my chores. For failing first year High School, for getting into repeated trouble at High School, for running away from home and for pretending to go to Marching Girls on Saturday afternoon when I was really just wandering around. And, later when I became an active and conscious hater and resister, I was beaten for being insolent and giving lip.

It would go like this. "I'll need to tell your father about this so you'd better go to your room and wait till he gets home." My mother was mostly on the side of the children but was also a mother of the times and believed in corporal punishment. She was a sweet, loving woman who was probably puzzled by the life she led. Our lives were significantly improved when she got herself a job at the wool factory. This meant that our pocket money increased fourfold and she herself was a lot happier because she was not reliant on the paternal paypacket to get the things she needed. Our food never improved though as she was a very basic cook.

So go to my room and try not to think about later. "Please let him not get home till after bedtime" would be my earnest whisper. So it might be a few hours and then I hear his car drive into the garage. I sweat and swallow. Then I hear the voices in the kitchen. A very short while later I hear the kitchen door bang and he would be shouting and swearing. Then up the hallway. There was no such thing as the neutral handing out of punishment. He would already be in a rage. I sit trembling on the side of the bed.

He rushes into the room, red faced and fills every corner with his frantic presence. I have already forgotten whatever my transgression was as the here and now is a huge adrenalin all encompassing and enveloping thing. I think I am enraged too. His belt comes off and is doubled over. He hauls me off the bed. He grabs me by the arm and I am pushed at a forward angle. The belt comes down on my legs and bottom. I cry and shake, I possibly shout and scream. It hurts very much but it is the shame and humiliation which hurts the most. I am powerless to do anything. He shouts as he whacks, humiliating swearing and other words of hate and anger which lodge in my brain more viciously than the physical beating. This happens more when he has had a few drinks. I have interfered with his plans for the evening.

Afterwards he lets go and I sob myself to sleep.

This was not the worst part of living with my father. If there were no beatings I still would have hated him just as readily.

He simply wasn't there as a human being. He inhabited the house with his non-humanness. When he wasn't home we were a reasonably content family. My mother chatted about her work mates and there was some laughter. We interacted as children do, scuffling and fighting and generally trying out who we were. There were chores to do which were done with the usual grumpiness. We played. We played a lot outside, riding our bikes, rolling our marbles, chasing and running, repairing and racing our dodgy go-karts, talking, playing and fighting with our street friends.

But when we saw or heard our father come home, it changed totally. We were reluctant to speak or act in any normal manner because this could be provoking. He rarely spoke at all except to chide. He did not seem to be in any way interested in our lives or be in any way involved in his own life. There was a wife and five children and it was completely alienating to him. On the rare occasions when we saw him with his adult friends the transformation was gob smacking. Who was this person who talked and laughed and was nice and friendly and seemed happy? If one of us plucked up any courage on these occasions to get into some of this happiness with him we would be brushed aside or made fun of. We didn't try to do this very often.

Every day held the same challenge. My father was usually in the house when we were preparing for school so breakfast was quickly gobbled down before any negative attention could be focused on us. Out of the house and off to school which was taken seriously by my big brother but not at all by me. My main preoccupation at school seemed to be to get into as much trouble as possible. I had a knack for being a trouble maker. I naturally chose friends who were also trouble makers. Such friends were probably as deeply unhappy and confused as I was but we never did speak of these things. Our aim was to assert any bits of ourselves which could be instantly retrieved and these were not the good bits. They were the raucous, insolent, uncooperative, resentful and sometimes bullying bits of ourselves. One or two teachers tried to get under my skin but I had every possible weapon to make sure these attempts were either unsuccessful or thoroughly counterproductive.

Studying, behaving in class, doing homework, being interested in any school subjects was just not on. So first year High School was a complete disaster and I was kept back for a repeat year. Second year High School was most assuredly a repeat of first year except that I decided to sit in the back of every class and read my way through the "Angelique" books. Complete trash but riveting to an immature, unhappy, escapist thirteen year old. I also had nasty little habit of composing tricky questions for some of my teachers who I had assessed as being fair game. I would look up from my book – the teachers seemed to have no power to stop this activity – and hold my arm up. My question usually had absolutely nothing to do with whatever was going on in class and mostly had the desired effect of causing major class disruption and sometimes a trip to the Headmaster's office.

My best friend in second year High School was Merlene Fawdry. We were so bad for each other but perfect as well. She has written a book about her childhood called "The Little Mongrel" and I now know that her childhood was much more terrifyingly unhappy than mine, although the details are different. We ran away together on one memorable occasion. She gives an account of this in her book. I am Jill. As ever we didn't share many confidences about our lives at home. We were far too busy trying to build up our self esteem in any way possible. We were children trying to stamp something of ourselves on the world to prove that we existed apart from the miserable bits which had to be endured.

In the afternoons when we got home from school we could play for a bit in the street or the backyard or the church grounds next door. My mother got home from her job a bit later and that was always welcome as we could then access the rest of the house. We were only allowed in the kitchen when there were no parents at home. Indeed, the kitchen door was locked as for some reason we were not considered trustworthy. My room was my reading place. I did read an enormous amount but suspect it was mostly of the "Angelique" variety when it wasn't comics. Disney were my favourites. Donald Duck loomed large.

My father was often late for tea, particularly when he was a Detective. They all drank together every night after work. He did come home by about 6 or 7 on weeknights and, if we had been congregating in the kitchen, we fled off to our bedrooms or to the lounge room which was a less safe bolt hole but ok for a short period until he finished his tea which had been warming and hardening in the oven.

Friday nights we were left unfed as this was the treat night when fish and chips would be brought home for us. Unfortunately, much more often than not, my father would not get in until 8 or 9 by which time the fish and chips were cold and inedible or we had all given up and gone to bed.

When I was about 11 or 12 I had a bad bike accident and spent six weeks in hospital which was utter bliss until I came home on crutches. From this time I remember a solitary event which is my only memory of my father being pleasant to me during my entire childhood. On my first morning home I hobbled out of my bedroom and made it to the kitchen. The only person there was my father. I hobbled to the pantry and looked helplessly at bread and vegemite. I turned around and looked at my father. He looked back at me, astonishment appearing momentarily on his face. "You sit down" he said, "I will get you your breakfast". And he did.

I did provoke my father. I was a smart aleck with a fiery mouth. This got worse as I got older and more confident.

I was finally expelled from school, much to my relief and, in all likelihood to the relief of the school. Now I could earn some money and become independent.

I was fourteen years old.

My first job was at a wool factory, not the one my mother worked at and, thankfully, not on the factory floor. I was employed, strangely and unaccountably, in the laboratory at Kelsall and Kemp. My day started at 7.30 and I was picked up by my pleasant young boss at 7 and driven to work. He also dropped me off after work at 4 and occasionally employed me as a baby sitter which was really good as the children were excellent sleepers and he always left me chocolate to eat while I watched TV.

I liked my boss and I liked my job. The job mainly involved dyeing bits of wool in various shades in order to develop dye formulae for large batches. I was the mixer upper and the stirrer and the timer and the watcher. I didn't have to do very much else and my boss was happy for me to read a book while still tending to my duties so long as nothing went wrong. Occasionally I was allowed to do the PH testing of the boiler. This was a good day when this happened. I made some friends at the factory, particularly a Quasimodo type young man who seemingly lived in the upper reaches of the wool sheds. He and I went to Saturday Westerns at the Star theatre every now and then.

I worked there for maybe a bit over a year, my pay packet was good for a young'un but then it all fell apart. My boss went on leave and I was supervised by a man who seemed to flat out hate me with a vengeance. He 'caught' me reading a book one day and sacked me on the spot. As with school expulsion at fourteen, summary sacking was presumably not illegal in the sixties.

My next job was in a shoe store in George St. Again I liked my boss and I didn't mind the work even though I was not very adept at tying shoelaces. There were a few of us working in the shop and we had a little tearoom out the back amongst the shoe boxes where the most marvelous conversations were held. It was usually the older women chatting and me listening.

I was able to walk to work although the distance seems rather far and hilly to me now. Every week I had my hair set as I was becoming a right little Miss. I bought clothes and I think I might have paid my mother some Board but can't be sure about this. I didn't make friends easily but I had a boyfriend called 'Radish.' We became engaged which was really very odd as we had no physical attraction to each other at all. Indeed, we became disengaged when he announced that he was in love with Graeme Murphy the Australian dancer. I am unsure as to whether Graeme Murphy ever knew about this.

Life at home continued much as before. I was earning minimal wages as a junior so the prospect of leaving home was as far away as it had been when I was at school. I had developed some fake confidence in relation to my father as it had been some considerable time since I had transgressed to the point of getting a hiding. I could enrage him in an instant with a smart aleck remark or a sniffy look but generally we stayed out of each other's way as much as possible. The misery continued to surround us all. My father had lost his job as a detective. The story is hazy but my understanding is that he was caught taking bribes. He became a travelling salesman for some product or other which required him to be away from home on overnight trips, sometimes even longer. These were happy punctuation marks in our lives but served to provide a painful contrast to the times when he was at home. Ray and I had always been the main targets. Graham and Sandra largely escaped his venom and dissatisfaction with the world. Leanne escaped it completely.

I hated him. Violence was never far beneath the surface. One weekend violence erupted again. It is not within my powers of recall to say how it started but I do know that I responded to him with insolence, either some muttered insult or a vicious gaze. He erupted immediately, this time as an adult rather than a punishing father. He pushed me up against the wall with his elbow cutting off my airflow. I sputtered and gasped while he pushed and pushed, going redder in the face all the while. He was out of control completely and could possibly have ended my life then if my mother hadn't rushed to my aid and got him away from me.

This shocked me and I brooded for some time, for some days, possibly weeks and then made a decision of sorts.

I would shoot him and life would change for the better.

6. Launceston

He had a rifle in his wardrobe. I had learned how to shoot a rifle when on holidays at Anson's Bay. A teenage friend of the family had taken me to the bush on a few occasions to shoot rabbits and wallabies. We never hit anything that we knew of but had a great deal of fun trying.

On Saturday 6th July 1963 I was in the house by myself. My father was out with Leanne somewhere and I knew they would be back soon. I went to his wardrobe and took out the rifle. I took it to my bedroom where I loaded it then I just sat. I was really really scared. Mainly I was scared of what I was about to do but I was more scared of not doing it. One significant reason for being scared of not doing it was the likelihood that he would find out I had taken the rifle and his anger would be boundless. I was therefore committed to a course of action which had occurred to me but which now had me in its grip. I sat on the bed for what seemed a very long time. I was just sitting, maybe trembling, frightened and charged with waves of adrenaline.

I heard voices and stood up. My father and Leanne had come into the house and were in the kitchen. I had not really thought about Leanne and whether I was putting her in danger and I didn't think about it then either. I was mainly worried about my own precarious position. I knew that my father would probably be in the kitchen for a little while as he would be preparing food or drink for them. I lifted the rifle and tucked it against myself then walked down the hallway as quietly as I could. The door to the kitchen was open and I turned in. My father was at the sink with his back to me and I lifted the rifle and pulled the trigger.

He shouted something and fell to the floor instantly. I dropped the rifle and went through the kitchen to the back door. I saw Leanne who was saying very clearly: "Shirley shot Daddy." I did not look at my father again and went out the back door, down the path, into the street and into the neighbours' house next door.

I knocked on the door and, when it was answered, I said, "I've just shot Dad. Can you call an ambulance?"

I was exhausted and exhilarated. The police came and I was taken to the police station where I made an impression of sorts by being cool and flippant and slightly weird.

The reality of it all began to seep in when I was finally locked in a police cell for the night. The cell was horrible. An open toilet in one corner, an unadorned stone or cement floor and a mattress stuffed with some rough scratchy material and covered in a sort of brown sugar bag. It was unheated and I lay on the 'bed' covered with the single blanket provided until my mother arrived. She came into the cell, looked at me and burst into tears. She said, "I'm sorry, I should have left him years ago." I loved her so much when she said that. She then just held me until they made her leave. I was given a cup of tea and possibly something to eat and then I slept.

The next morning I met my defence counsel, Reg. Hall who walked me through what was to happen next – just say, "I plead not guilty and wish to reserve my defence.'

After that first brief court hearing, during which bail was granted, I went home with my mother.

The next few months were really quite interesting and fairly enjoyable. I decided that I would resign from my job and live on the 'dole'. After all, I needed to be available for reasonably frequent meetings with professional luminaries such as my lawyer and my psychiatrist. I didn't much enjoy the lawyer meetings, not so much because of being asked to 'recall' things but more because I was often being persuaded against my will to agree to particular slants, emphases and interpretations. I still bathed myself in an air of unreality and could only be brought briefly into the real world if my lawyer became impatient with my tendency towards the moral high ground, reminding me that I could actually end up in jail for a fairly long time.

I did, however, enjoy the meetings with my psychiatrist, for a while anyway. He asked me to write the story of my life which I finished in a couple of days and handed to him with a flourish. It was about two pages long. He grimaced and said he wanted at least 100 pages. He never did get them and, to this day, I am not sure what the purpose of this request was. I was also subjected to a battery of tests, intelligence, personality and the like. I really liked doing these as it was sufficiently remote from my present reality and I always seemed to be able to surprise him. I had announced early on that I was a lesbian even though, after further questioning, I had to admit that my experiences were strictly in the realms of fantasy. He seemed to take this as a personal affront and began a campaign of – as he described it – getting me to understand that men can be nice. This campaign, I soon realized, was to revolve solely around him even though he was a middle aged unattractive balding and overweight chap. He insisted that I travel with him to Hobart for something, further tests of some kind, and on the way back fairly late in the evening he pulled off the side of the road and put his arm around me. I found it intolerably oppressive and held my breath for the longest time. He did little else except murmer at me as he cradled me closer to his quite unlovely self. If this was therapy or even some kind of anti-gay mini-intervention then it utterly failed. I couldn't wait to escape from his cloying embrace and I never, ever let myself be at risk of such an encounter again.

I was fully confirmed as a lesbian.

Life at home was good. My father was in the Austin Hospital in Melbourne and I wasn't to see him again for over a year. He was paralysed from the waist down and, callous as I remained to his plight, my main thought about this was that it would be very difficult for him to terrorise me, my mother or my brother from a wheelchair.

I did get a job of sorts. I had become a bit of a beatnik, wearing black stockings and huge amounts of black eyeliner. I had decided I would like to be an artist so my job was as a cleaner at the Mary Jolliffe Art Gallery. She promised me that in return for cleaning she would give me art lessons. I didn't clean very well but she didn't teach very well either so we were quits. During this time I became acquainted with her best friend Mrs Lazenby, mother of Nigel Lazenby, now a well respected Tasmanian artist. I really like Nigel but I fell in love with his mother. One would think I would have some notion of what her first name was but it is not to be...

I spent a fair bit of time with them as they lived not far away from my home and also because their home was welcoming and filled with light and warmth. I assumed they didn't know who I 'was' until one day Nigel mentioned casually: "You know, I read somewhere that many teenagers think about trying to kill one or the other of their parents." As he was about my age I initially thought he was talking about some deep seated hatred for his mother and then the penny dropped and I realized I had been sussed. It didn't make much difference and we continued to be friends right up until the trial. After the trial I never saw them again.

In November 1963 trial day arrived. I was persuaded to drop the black stockings and eyeliner for a conservative new outfit but I insisted on wearing sunglasses.

The trial was fairly fully reported in the three main Tasmanian newspapers. I have chosen to include the complete report from the Launceston Examiner as this is one closest to home.

I had gone through the previous 4-5 months in a little cloud cuckoo land of my own, occasionally being brought down to earth by my lawyer, but largely unconcerned about the outcome of the trial. If I thought about it at all, it was to conclude that if I went to jail, I must have deserved it and, if I didn't, I had no idea what I was going to do. Jail at least was a reality.

The trial had started on a Wednesday and continued through to the following Tuesday.

On Friday afternoon, at the conclusion of the day's business, everything changed.

My lawyer asked me and my mother to come to his office as a letter had been delivered to him that afternoon and we should urgently read it.

It read:

"Mr Reginald G. Hall

Solicitor

17a Welman St

Launceston

Dear Mr Hall,

After reading the newspaper-reports of Shirley Ann Gibbons' ordeal, my Husband and myself, after serious and deep consideration, came to the decision that we would like to assist her, with every means at our disposal, to forget the pain and sorrow of her past, and help her build a new life.. – If this would entail helping her finish her studies, and gain a University degree, we would stand by her morally and financially. If she prefers to take a job, and make herself a new life, we would help her, guide her, provide her with a home and loving kindness – in short, give her the type of care and love every young girl should be entitled to.

We feel we are more than capable of doing this – providing of course, that Shirley herself is willing to accept our help and love -. We have no children. Our baby daughter died two years ago. Myself, am of Continental birth, with a Uni. Degree from my home town. Soon after my arrival in Tasmania, in the early 50s I took an Arts Course in History and Geography at the University of Hobart – so I feel confident that I can help and guide Shirley, should she choose to continue her schooling. Coming from the Continent, I also have a deep sense of family loyalty and respect ingrained in me. This respect, love and loyalty, would now include Shirley too. We have a home at 110 Elphin Rd., run by my Mother, a highly intelligent and educated old lady, who is wholeheartedly with us in this scheme.

My husband is a well-known Launceston businessman, born in Tasmania. He owns, and at the present runs, this Hotel, one of Launceston's largest. Our marriage is marked by deep happiness and understanding, and might help Shirley to gain the right idea about human relationships. He is also wonderful with children and young people, and wishes with all his heart to be of some service now, when help is so obviously needed.

Will you please give our offer your best consideration, if possible discuss it with Shirley, and call us please as soon as we can be of help. You can reach us at the Hotel by contacting us or leaving a message on 22421. – If you think it would be possible for me to see Shirley tomorrow – or at any time, please let me know. It might help her to know, that, even now, we love her, and want to be her friends.

Our offer, needless to say, holds good, whatever the outcome of the trial. Our only request is to remain totally anonymous, under no circumstances our names to be made public, although, if it helps please mention it at the trial (without names of course), that home, help and guiding for the future is awaiting Shirley when she is free again."

[final part of letter lost]

This letter was signed Charles and Éva Castley.

We arranged to meet at the Cornwall Hotel on Saturday afternoon. It was a brief meeting. Everyone, presumably, was nervous. The result of this for me was that I was stand-offish. My potential new father was warm and brisk. My potential new mother was beautiful, trailed a cloud of perfume and talked of the future: school; University; a new family. I said little, except that I couldn't make a decision then but must consult my lawyer!

I went home and curled up on the couch in the lounge room. Until that afternoon I had not cared one whit about the outcome of the trial. Suddenly I seemed to care deeply as an actual, positive future had suddenly been glimpsed. I cried for a long time and started to HOPE.

My potential new mother had displayed extraordinary courage and resilience all her life. Being a self centred brat, I did not then realize what an act of courage is was for her to want to take a completely unknown teenager into her home. The one known fact was that I had shot my father.

The other completely selfless and courageous act was the willingness of my natural mother to give me a chance at a new life.

The weekend passed eventually. Monday was summing up day. Tuesday was decision day. The Judge's final comments to the jury were explicit and the jury returned within about an hour with a Not Guilty verdict and I was free.

My life was about to turn around in an astonishing way.

I returned to school. This was not all that easy as none of the private schools would accept me. Broadland House and Methodist Ladies' College were of one mind and that was that I was a good candidate for 'reform school' but not for them, thank you. Eventually my mother pulled some strings through a local priest and I was accepted at Sacred Heart College. As I had left High School at the end of second year, and hadn't actually learned anything in any of the years I was at High School, enrolling in Matriculation was a bit of an ask.

It was a small class of about 12 girls and I was instantly adopted by the resident daggy God-botherer. The rest of them preferred to bide their time. I embarrassed myself quite a bit during the early weeks, not so much because of my ignorance but because I became unduly excited about such matters as photosynthesis which was a yawn to the rest of the class. I announced proudly to my mother one evening that I had decided to 'do' Matriculation over two years instead of one year and would therefore drop French and Modern History. This decision remained in place for all of the minute it took me to announce it. French and Modern History were quickly reinstated. I was not really lagging in Ancient History, Modern History or English as much of the subject matter was specifically new for everyone. I was appallingly behind in French and Biology and would probably not have made it except that my mother, in addition to building me as a person from scratch, sat with me every night for hours teaching me, making me work, ensuring I spent as much time as possible simply catching up. And, of course, it helped that she was fluent in French, unlike Sister Bridget, the French teacher.

My new grandmother spoke with a fairly strong accent. She had learned English when she was in her fifties. I think she found me to be a most peculiar person but she coped with her daughter's project quite well. We eventually became firm friends. One evening when I was having the usual struggle trying to sort out the French word for 'hat' or 'cow', my mother said "You will forget Matriculation one day," and my grandmother said laconicly, "I never did." I suspect my mother had a word with her later about undoing all her good work.

My grandmother was amazingly talented. She could sew, embroider, paint and cook. The Hungarian National Gala Dress which she did make for my mother when she was in her seventies is now on display in the National Museum of Australia.

Her secret recipe for Sachertorte is heaven, if you have the patience. Here it is:

Excerpt from letter written by my mother to me in 1980

"MUST BE DONE EXACTLY LIKE THIS

150gm unsalted butter and 150gm caster sugar beaten till frothy;

add 6 egg yolks and during continuous mixing add slowly 150 gm melted chocolate and 120 gm flour, in the end the hard-beaten 6 egg whites (fold in only). Bake in greased papered tins in the oven (400 F). ONLY 2/3rd is baked, the remaining 1/3rd keep for filling and overglazing. If preferred, can put one layer of apricot jam between the cake-layers, or alternatively, glaze the cake with chocolate. But it is best filled and glazed with its own mixture, especially if you serve in separate bowl vanilla-ed beaten cream with it.

Next page:

"There is an official recipe from Time-Life books which is supposed to be ah, so good. But your Mama said arrrgh! What sort of gonk is THAT? So here goes her SECRET recipe to be guarded with your life. TOTALLY SECRET. So much so, that the most important item cannot be ever written into it, in case it falls into heathen hands. That is, that instead of the 120gm flour you in fact add 6 tablespoons lady-finger crumbs. You buy the ladyfingers biscuits, and in a grater, or mixer you crumb a few biscuits medium rough – not too fine. Add six tablespoons into the mixture INSTEAD of the 120gm plain flour... Do not forget."

Mostly that first year my mother talked. She built me with words. Of course there were the usual group interactions, meal times, etc. But whenever she had me on her own, which was homework time and bed time, she talked.

I don't remember the substance just the flavour and purpose which was to build my confidence, build my character, build my motivation, build my optimism, build my courage and build my belief in myself. She was proud of all I did, no matter how small. Of course, I threw the occasional tantrum. Nothing fazed her, she just talked more and loved me more.

I got rid of the God-botherer and started to mingle more widely in class. Everyone was a prefect except me which was annoying but I got over it.

The year ground to an end. 'Speech night' arrived and it was announced that I was Dux of the school. My mother leapt to her feet in the crowded auditorium and shouted "That's my daughter!" She was SO proud. I was mortified.

That Summer, my new mother and I went to visit my paralysed father.

He had not returned to the family home. My mother had sold it and moved to Sydney with her three youngest children and he had moved into a house in Derby where he had grown up so as to be near his parents.

He was waiting in the yard in his wheelchair when we arrived. He smiled and looked happy to see us, then took us on a guided tour of his house. The highlight for him was his matching bread bin and canisters which he said was just lucky but he was very pleased. We had a cup of tea and some biscuits and he asked questions about school, about what I would be doing at University and my driving lessons. My mother did most of the talking and, as always, was charming and entertaining. It couldn't have been pleasant for her but she took it in her stride. I was dazed to say the least. Who was this person?

He chatted, spoke quietly, made small jokes, was self effacing, polite and pleasant.

He seemed happy. He certainly seemed happier than I had ever seen him. He kissed me when we left.

On the drive back I tried to talk to my mother about him. I felt terribly guilty that she must have thought I really was a monster for shooting such a nice man and pretending that I had done it because he was a vicious brute. She understood, naturally, and simply said "For some reason he too was desperately unhappy."

Some years later he wrote me a letter. It is the only one he ever wrote.

"Main St

Derby

17.7.67

Dear Shirley

Received your letter about a fortnight ago. I suppose you will be very busy with your studies. I hope you don't find it too hard getting your degree. I was surprised to hear Ray had been over, does he still go to school. I haven't had a letter from Sydney for a good while now. I wrote to Graeme a long time back and said I would pay his and Leanne's fares for the Sept holidays and asked him to find out the cost but he hasn't let me know yet. I have been getting a room painted out for them and have ordered more furniture for it so it will be nice for them. It's been teeming with rain here for a few days so I have been inside most of the time, when it's not too cold I go on the front verandah, the old verandahs might be old fashioned but they are handy this weather. I do a fair bit of reading and swap books around with a few others. Has the adoption business been all fixed up yet. Love Dad xxx"

I cried when I read it, perhaps because it could have been from someone I met in the street.

My father died of a heart attack shortly after he wrote this.

7. The Trial

EXAMINER newspaper Thursday November 14th 1963

GIRL ADMITTED PLANNING SHOT AT FATHER

A detective told a jury in the Launceston Supreme Court yesterday that in 12 year's experience he had not seen a female behave at an interview like a girl on trial for attempting to murder her father.

He said the girl had told him the shooting of her father was "fully premeditated" and "if he isn't dead, it's just too bad."

The detective said the girl had a look of intense hatred in her eyes during the interview.

The girl is Shirley Anne Gibbons (17), shop assistant, of Lanoma St., Launceston.

She pleaded not guilty to charges of the attempted murder of her father, Cyril Edward Gibbons, at Launceston on July 6, and committing an act intended to cause grievous bodily harm to Cyril Edward Gibbons.

The trial, before Mr. Justice Crawford, is not expected to end until tomorrow.

Mr. R.G.Hall is appearing for Miss Gibbons, and Mr. J.B.Hutchins is prosecuting.

Outlining the Crown case against Miss Gibbons, Mr. Hutchins told the jury it was alleged that the girl shot her father in the back with a .22 rifle while he was preparing a bottle for his 2 year old baby.

SPINAL INJURY

Gibbons, he said, had been shot in the lower spine.

He was paralysed from the waist down and might be in that state for the rest of his life.

Mr. Hutchins alleged that Miss Gibbons shot her father because of her hatred for him.

Det.-Sen.-Const. D.J.Fenton told the jury that he went to a house at 22 Lanoma St. about 3.10pm. on Saturday, July 6.

A man now known to him as Cyril Edward Gibbons was lying on his back on the kitchen floor with his feet towards the sink and his head towards the hall doorway.

During a short conversation with Gibbons, he saw a .22 rifle lying on the hall floor opposite the kitchen door.

Soon afterwards he and Sen.-Const. Policewoman W. Godfrey accompanied Miss Gibbons to the Police Station, where she was interviewed about 3.30pm.

Miss Gibbons told them she was 16.

Asked whether she was feeling "okay", she replied: "Charming".

'MELODRAMATIC'

Det. Fenton said that after warning Miss Gibbons and asking her if she understood the warning, she said: "Yes, very melodramatic, isn't it?"

Told that her father said he was "fixing" a bottle for the baby at the kitchen sink when he heard a shot, she replied: "Only heard it? Didn't he feel it?"

Det. Fenton said Miss Gibbons told him that she had shot her father with the rifle and she had added, "I hardly think Leanne could have."

She told him that Leanne was her baby sister.

She said she had got the rifle from her father's bedroom and the bullet from a case in her room.

Det. Fenton said he asked Miss Gibbons if she had been fully conscious of what she was doing when she shot her father.

She had replied: "It was fully premeditated, don't worry."

In reply to further questions, she told him that she had not really intended to kill her father.

"If he isn't dead, it's just too bad. If he had died, I wouldn't worry much either", Det. Fenton said Miss Gibbons told him.

Asked if something had happened between her and her father, Miss Gibbons replied: "Something? Miss Godfrey

knows. Since I was born he hasn't said one kind word."

'LOST COURAGE'

She said that she had decided to shoot her father "quite a while ago" but her courage had failed.

Det. Fenton said Miss Gibbons had gone on: "Last weekend he was ranting on about unimportant things and I decided that if he did it again that would be it.

"Today he went mad about the washing up and I had had enough of him.

"He is only a blot on the earth, anyway."

Det. Fenton said that Miss Gibbons wrote a statement with a pen and signed it, after appearing to read the statement.

The alleged statement was then produced and read to the jury by a court officer.

It read: "Does a person need any specific reason other than hate, loathing disgust for removing something that has done no good whatsoever in his lifetime and is never likely to?

"he is a bully and a coward, a sadist and also an extremely stupid man. Anything bad or rotten that I have ever done or had done to me has been directly or indirectly related to him.

"If it hadn't been for the shadow he cast over my life when I was in high school I would have got my matriculation and gone to uni., far away from anything concerned with him.

"I hope I never have to lower myself to look at his odious body ever again.

"If he had left me alone, if he had let everybody alone and gone his own drunken, loathsome way instead of trying to act 'big boss', he wouldn't be where he is now.

"There's nothing much else I can say except that I am glad I had the courage to do it.

NO COMPLAINT

Det. Fenton said that after the interview at the police station, Miss Gibbons told Insp.L.W.H.Rothwell that the statement was hers and that she had no complaint about the treatment of her by the police.

About 4.25pm., Miss Gibbons, Miss Godfrey and he returned to the house in Lanoma St. where the accused showed him where she obtained the rifle and bullet.

Det. Fenton said Miss Gibbons also showed him where she had been standing when her father was shot.

Under cross examination, Det. Fenton said the girl had behaved entirely contrary to what he normally expected from a young girl. During the interview at the police station, he had noticed she had "a look of intense hatred in her eyes when she referred to her father, and spoke with a cynical twist of her lips."

"The unusual thing was that she did not show any emotion – that is, she had no inclination to cry, or anything I would normally expect from a female," Det. Fenton said.

"I have been in the police force for about twelve years, eight of them as a detective, and have had a great deal of experience of interviewing young girls.

"I have never seen a female behave like this girl," he said.

Asked by Mr. Hall whether Miss Gibbons' behaviour had been "automatic," Det. Fenton said it had not. He denied that she had been "aloof" from what was going on at the interview.

Mr. Hall: "I suggest that, considering the circumstances, particularly the age of the girl, you rushed into the interview with considerable haste?"

Det. Fenton: "The girl never gave me a chance to slow down the interview."

Mr. Hall: "Did she tender the idea that the interview would not be fair to her?" – "No."

"Or was it your idea to strike while the iron was hot?" – "It is a detective's duty always to strike while the iron is hot."

In re-examination by Mr. Hutchins, Det. Fenton said he was satisfied that the girl was in a fit state to be interviewed.

Mrs. Frances Mary Burgess, now of Smithton, but formerly of Lanoma St., said she lived next door to the Gibbonses on July 6.

HEARD SOUND

That afternoon she had been in the kitchen when she heard what sounded like a shot. A few minutes later, Shirley Ann Gibbons came round the back of the house and said to her, "Will you please ring the ambulance Mrs. Burgess? I just shot dad."

Mrs. Burgess said she asked whether it was true and Miss Gibbons said "Yes."

Mrs. Burgess said her husband then called out from the yard of the Gibbons' residence and she took the baby Leanne from over the fence, and rang the police and ambulance.

In answer to Mr. Hall she said Miss Gibbons' face was very grey and expressionless and her hands were straight at her sides. Her fingers were stiff.

Ronald Clyde Burgess said he had been in his back yard on the afternoon of July 6 when he heard a crack like a rifle shot. He had not taken much notice as he was listening to a Wireless.

He then heard someone call out but did not take much notice. He then heard a second call and recognized his neighbour, Mr. Gibbons, calling out, "Are you there Ron?"

JUMPED FENCE

He said he jumped the fence and went into the kitchen of Gibbons' home. He saw Mr. Gibbons lying on the floor. He picked up the baby and passed her over the fence to his wife.

"I did not touch anything in the house and waited for the police to come," he said.

The hearing will continue at 10 a.m. today.

EXAMINER newspaper Friday November 15th 1963

GIRL TOLD OF 'LONG YEARS' OF FAMILY HIDINGS

A 17-year old girl, charged with the attempted murder of her father on July 6, described how members of her family and herself had been mentally and physically beaten by her father over a number of years, in a statement read to Launceston Supreme Court yesterday.

The statement read by her counsel (Mr. R. G. Hall), related how at the age of 13 she had been severely beaten with a thick billet of firewood, and how, a few days before the alleged shooting, her father had "almost choked" her at home.

The girl – Shirley Ann Gibbons of Lanoma St., Launceston – has pleaded not guilty to a charge of attempting to murder her father, Cyril Edward Gibbons, on July 6 and to an alternative charge of committing an act intended to cause grievous bodily harm.

The Crown evidence was completed soon after the luncheon adjournment yesterday with evidence from Policewoman Sen.-Const. W. Godfrey.

Mr. J. B. Hutchins is prosecuting.

"DIDN'T CARE"

Const. Godfrey said the girl's attitude during an interview at the police station soon after the shooting "had seemed to convey that she'd done what was right and didn't care about it."

Under cross examination by Mr. Hall, Miss Godfrey said the girl was not nervous or trembling in the slightest degree during the interview.

"She seemed quite calm and gave an impression of being quite sure of herself," Miss Godfrey said.

She had found Miss Gibbons very different to most people in the same circumstances. The majority shook, broke down and cried.

Some became "cheeky" to police, while many young girls asked for their mothers. Miss Gibbons had not done any of these things.

She had seen the girl several years ago after her (Miss Gibbons') father resigned from the police force.

She could not remember having seen bruises on the girl's body at the time or having been told that the bruises had been caused by her having been beaten by a thick piece of wood.

"SOME TROUBLE"

However, she could recollect some sort of trouble between the girl and her father.

Miss Godfrey said she knew the father quite well but could not recall ever having been in his company "off the job."

Yesterday was the second day of the hearing which is expected to end today.

On Wednesday the jury heard evidence from Det.-Sen.-Const. D. J. Fenton of an interview with the girl at Launceston police station, in which he said she admitted shooting her father, and made a statement.

He also gave evidence of having taken possession of a rifle which, he alleged, she had admitted using to shoot her father in the back.

Sen.-Const. Eaves said in evidence before Mr. Justice Crawford yesterday that the .22 model rifle which he had been handed by

Det. Fenton for examination was notoriously unsafe.

The rifle was made at Lithgow, N. S. W. and against a trigger pull of 5lb. to 7lb. for other .22 rifles, that particular model had a trigger pull of only 3lb. 2ozs.

That was excessively light and abnormal, he said.

Const. Eaves told Mr. Hutchins that he could find no finger prints on the rifle.

The barrel was slightly rusted on the exterior, and the whole rifle was covered with fine dust," he said.

These conditions affected finger printing.

RIFLE TESTS

He had tested the rifle and found it very prone to accidental firing.

The rifle had fired under tests when he had:

. Not cocked the rifle, but given the cocking knob a slight blow with a 2lb. rubber mallet;

. Cocked the rifle, and dropped it butt first on to a hard surface from about 1ft;

. Cocked the rifle and struck it with the mallet at various points on the exterior, including the butt, stock and other parts.

Const. Eaves told Mr. Hutchins that he had also examined a green sweater with a hole in the centre of the back, consistent with a hole made by a .22 bullet, but had found no trace of burn or powder marks on it.

At the conclusion of the Crown case, Mr. Hall read a prepared statement, signed by Miss Gibbons.

Miss Gibbons did not give sworn evidence.

Miss Gibbons' statement read:

"I, Shirley Ann Gibbons, state as follows: I reached the age of 17 years on October 15 this year.

"Ever since I can remember I have lived in fear of my father. This fear became much more intense when, at the age of 11, I witnessed a brutal attack which he made on my mother.

"Although I was horrified at what was happening to my mother, I can still remember my own terror at the thought of what he might do to me and the other children. The police came to the house.

"**After that incident, my father showed that he was aware of my fear of him, and he displayed a spiteful and sadistic attitude towards me.**

"He also frequently behaved violently towards my mother and especially towards my elder brother.

"He always used really obscene language to us on every occasion when he lost his temper or was merely in a bad mood. He had a violent temper and often flew into a mad rage for no reason at all. He was worse after he had been drinking, which happened frequently.

SCHOOL INTEREST

"There was never any happiness in the home when he was there. It was a place of misery and tension. We all tried to keep out of his presence as much as possible.

"Despite my unhappy home life, I took a great deal of interest in my school work at first and was doing very well, being two years younger than the average age in my class, and entered high school when I was 11, but then my work began to deteriorate.

"When I was 12, I had a fall from my bicycle and fractured my skull and severely lacerated my leg.

"After I recovered, I seemed to be out of touch with everything and my school work deteriorated still further.

"When I was 13, my father gave me a severe beating with a thick billet of firewood. I have been quite unable to remember what led to this beating, or what immediately followed it, and I know these things only from what my mother has told me.

"But I do know that I left home the next day and stayed with another girl and slept in the Gorge Reserve. I was found and brought home by the police, who warned my father against ill-treating me again.

"From that time my father usually made a show of ignoring me completely during his calmer periods. For example, on all of the many occasions when he has overtaken me in his car when I have been walking to work, sometimes in the rain, he has passed me by. But he frequently spoke abusively of me to my mother in my hearing. He spoke to me directly only when he was in a rage or when he found an opportunity to say something particularly cutting or insulting.

"On many of these occasions he told me to leave the home.

"When I turned 14, I obtained exemption from school so that I could work and earn enough to enable me to leave home. However, I had to continue to live at home while my wages were still low.

"In August of last year I saw another assault which my father made on my mother. In a fit of temper he had thrown a dinner set on the garbage tin. When my mother spoke to him about it, he attacked her. She had to have medical treatment. I was very frightened and upset by this incident.

"GRABBED ME"

"On the Sunday before the 6th of July this year I was sitting in the kitchen reading. I heard my father raising his voice in the lounge. He strode into the kitchen and asked: 'Has your mother told you to make your bed?' I said: 'Yes.'

"He then said, 'Get in and make it,' and grabbed me by the shoulder and pulled me off my chair and threw me against the kitchen cupboard. I ran into the hall and called him a coward. He came after me, grabbed me again, pushed me against the wall, and forced his forearm against my throat so that I could not breathe.

"He held me in that way until my mother came from the lounge and made him let go. He released me and I staggered into my room and fell on the bed.

"On the evening of Friday July 5th, my father was at home. My two-and-a-half year old sister Leanne, was not feeling well and was crying. My father suddenly yelled, 'For God's sake, shut up,' and lashed out with his hand and sent her flying across the room. This upset me greatly.

TRIED READING

"On Saturday July 6th, I went to work feeling very depressed. I returned home for lunch about noon. As I was walking along the hall to the bathroom, I accidentally collided with my father at the corner in the hall. He turned around and glared at me and grunted. I think that there was some other trouble with him that day, but I have been unable to remember what it was.

"I know that I went to my bedroom and remained there for a long time. I remember that I tried to read, but could not.

"But I had a strange restless feeling. I felt tired of life and hopeless. I felt that my life was a failure and I could not bear to face the future.

"I felt the same as I did on a previous occasion a few months earlier when I had taken my father's rifle with an idea of shooting myself in the head, but found that I could not do so. I started to tremble violently, and, as far as I can remember, I continued to shake for what I think must have been several hours.

LOADED RIFLE

"I remember going into the main bedroom to get the rifle and loading it with a bullet which had been in a box in my room for some years.

"I cannot remember just when I did this, but I know that it was during a period in the afternoon when my father was away from the house with Leanne.

"I have tried to remember what I had in mind at the time I got the rifle, but I cannot. I know that I was still shaking and put the rifle on the bed.

"I felt mentally and physically exhausted and I could not stop the shaking, which seemed to become worse when I tried to stop it.

"I have only a vague recollection of carrying the rifle as I walked along the hall to the kitchen door.

"I cannot remember whether I was still shaking as I walked along the hall but I do remember that as I stood in the kitchen doorway and saw my father standing at the sink, I was then shaking violently and my hands were clammy.

FATHER FELL

"I was then holding the rifle in one hand, my right hand. I know that I did not hold it in both hands. While I was standing in the doorway I heard the rifle go off. I cannot remember touching the trigger.

"I heard my father say 'Christ' and saw him fall backwards from the sink on to the radiator. The shot was still ringing in my ears.

"I walked unsteadily towards my room. I dropped the rifle somewhere. I saw Leanne. She spoke, but I do not know what she said. I think that I put my coat on; - I know that I felt terribly cold. I must have gone out the back door which is the usual way.

"The next thing I remember was being in the yard of the Burgess' house next door. I told Mrs. Burgess to phone for the ambulance and then I stood in the middle of their yard.

"Someone told me to sit in a car and I sat and waited until it was driven to the police station. I remember being asked questions and answering and writing a statement.

"Everything seemed unreal. I felt that it was not happening to me.

"FELT REMOTE"

"I felt remote from what was taking place and quite unconcerned about what might happen to me until I was locked in a cell. Looking back on it now, I do not know how I could have written the statement which I did write or have said the things I did say, although I can remember doing most of those things.

"I do not know why I took the rifle to the kitchen. I am quite certain that I did not intend to kill my father or cause him the terrible injury which he has suffered. I am unable to say positively that I did not touch the trigger inadvertently but I have no recollection of doing so and I think it unlikely that I did.

"**I feel sure that I would remember if I had pulled the trigger deliberately and I am certain that I would not have held the rifle**

only in one hand (as I know I did) if I intended to fire it.

"I had never fired the rifle before and I did not know that it was unsafe until I heard the evidence in the Police Court."

FORMED OPINION

Dr. R. C. Simpson, a psychiatrist at the Launceston General Hospital told the court he had examined the girl on a number of occasions since the alleged offence.

He had formed the opinion that she was a "hysterical personality." He explained this by saying that she had a tendency to split off pieces of consciousness.

"This is a tendency towards dissociation – or a person could almost become two people.

"They could dissociate all emotion from themselves in cases where emotion could be expected," Dr. Simpson said.

However he said he was not impressed with this feature at his first interview with Miss Gibbons on July 11th.

In subsequent interviews, he found that the girl had "abnormal hysterical personality."

"I have seen many statements by people confessing crime, but the girl's statement to the police in this instance was unique in my experience," he said.

"There was a complete absence of any self-preservation."

The hearing was adjourned to 10 a. m. today.

SMARTLY DRESSED FOR TRIAL

Miss Gibbons has sat throughout the trial without signs of any emotion. She has been smartly dressed in a blue and white check blouse and a teal blue pleated skirt.

Her hair, done in urchin style, is topped with a high-crowned, wide-brimmed white hat.

EXAMINER newspaper Saturday November 16th 1963

DOCTOR DEFENDS HIS OPINION OF L'TON GIRL

A psychiatrist denied in Launceston Supreme Court yesterday that he had been trying to find "some niche" like insanity or dissociation for the

defence of a girl on an attempted murder charge.

He said that at the time of the alleged offence he believed the girl was in a state of automatism and would not be in her usual state of consciousness.

The psychiatrist, Dr. R. C. Simpson, of Launceston, was the only witness called in the defence of Shirley Ann Gibbons (17), of Lanoma St., Launceston.

Miss Gibbons has pleaded not guilty to a charge of attempting to murder her father Cyril Edward Gibbons, on July 6, and to an alternative charge of committing an act intended to cause grievous bodily harm to Cyril Edward Gibbons.

Yesterday was the third day of the trial which was adjourned by Mr. Justice Crawford to 10 a.m. Monday.

Defence counsel (Mr. R. G. Hall) is only part way through his address to the jury.

On Thursday Mr. Hall tendered to the court a signed statement by Miss Gibbons which alleged beatings by her father.

Continuing his evidence Dr. Simpson said that in a discussion with Det.-Sen. Const. D. J. Fenton on Tuesday afternoon, before the trial, the word "automatic" had been used by him to describe the girl's behaviour at the time of the interview with the police.

'ABNORMAL USES'

Dr. Simpson said Det. Fenton had agreed with him that the word described her behaviour.

"The general run of the conversation was that her behaviour was unusual. I think abnormal was used in reference to her behaviour but I don't know who used it," he told Mr. Hall.

He said they both had agreed that the girl's statement was one of the most unusual they had both seen.

"I said it was unique in my experience."

Dr. Simpson said that results of tests on the girl showed a "disrythmin" condition, which could "possibly have been the result of a head injury she had described, or slight neuro-psychological instability."

He said this might have been a factor in facilitating the process of dissociation in the girl which he had described on Thursday.

Mr. Hall: "As a result of your tests and observations, what is your opinion as to her state at the time of the alleged offence?"

INVOLUNTARY

Dr. Simpson: "My opinion is that she was in a state of automatism. In such a state she would not be in her usual state of consciousness.

"Her behaviour would not be controlled by her will in such a state any more than it is in a dream," Dr. Simpson said.

A person in such a state would not have the power to repress or suppress actions. A person's actions in such a state would be involuntary.

He told Mr. Hall that in her normal state he did not think Miss Gibbons would commit an act of violence.

Cross-examined by the Senior Crown Prosecutor (Mr. J. B. Hutchins) Dr. Simpson said he had not been told of any acts of violence by the girl other than the one with which she was charged.

Mr. Hutchins: "What about the attempt at suicide?"

Dr. Simpson: "She did tell me she had considered shooting herself, and I believe

she went as far as handling the gun. She said she could not go on with it."

Asked by Mr. Hutchins if, in the conversation with Det. Fenton on Tuesday, he had compared Miss Gibbons with the English sexual murderer Christie, Dr. Simpson said: "We were discussing persons generally who were of a hysterical type. I mentioned that Christie was such a type. It was only a passing remark."

'AMMUNITION?'

Mr. Hutchins: "You reported certain parts of that conversation to Mr. Hall?"

Dr. Simpson: "Yes, I thought it was my duty as I thought it was another piece of evidence."

"You were not feeding Mr. Hall with ammunition to fire at Mr. Fenton?" – "Certainly not."

Dr. Simpson told Mr. Hutchins that he had first concluded that Miss Gibbons was in a state of automatism "mostly in the last week or so."

He denied Mr. Hutchins' suggestion that he had been trying to find "some niche" like insanity or dissociation in which to fit Miss Gibbons for a defence.

He also strongly denied a suggestion by Mr. Hutchins that he helped draft the girl's unsworn statement to fit in with what he found to be her "condition".

Asked what was his conviction on the girl's state of automatism at the time of the alleged incident, Dr. Simpson said he thought it was "highly probably." He would not go further.

Mr. Hutchins: "Could the crisis with the girl, in which she allegedly shot her father, occur again if the father returns home?"

Dr. Simpson: "It's very probable, although I should not think so. The state has spent itself to a great extent. Her present attitude I would say, is that her feelings have lost intensity as a result of what happened to the father."

"Because she achieved her purpose?"

"Because he is an invalid she feels differently."

"Don't you agree that on the whole of the police interview, there was no amnesia on her part."

Dr. Simpson: "Patchy amnesia. I'm not really concerned with that."

Mr. Hutchins: "But I am and the jury will be. What about the question to her at the interview, 'Were you fully conscious of what you were doing when you shot your father?' and her reply, 'It was fully premeditated, don't worry.' Is that likely to be the truth?"

DEFENCE POINTS

Dr. Simpson: "I think it fits in with the feeling she had had for some years and a state of auto-consciousness. It does not destroy my theory of automatism."

At the conclusion of Dr. Simpson's evidence, the defence closed its case.

In his address to the jury, Mr. Hall said the main points of the defence were that the girl was in a state of "automatism" at the time and that there was an accidental discharge of the rifle.

"It is not suggested by the defence that the girl was not holding the rifle which fired the bullet which hit Mr. Gibbons.

"The Crown says that the accused deliberately fired the rifle, pointing it at the father with the intention of killing him," Mr. Hall said.

He said that even if the whole of the Crown evidence was taken at face value it would be extremely difficult for the jury to say the charge was proved.

"Despite a lengthy interview by the police, only once was the word 'kill' or 'intention to kill' used at all. That was in answer to the question, 'Did you intend to kill him?' Her answer had been, 'Not really, if he isn't dead it's too bad…'" Mr. Hall said.

SOUGHT HELP

It was an answer by a girl apparently falling over herself to incriminate herself.

"If she had intended to kill, one would have expected some interest from her in finding out if she had. There was nothing in the statement taken at the interview to show she thought her father was dead or dying.

"The girl also went into the Burgess yard to ask for an ambulance. Surely, then, she was not hoping he was dead or would die, or believed he was dead," Mr. Hall said.

"She obviously believed he was injured and needed assistance."

Mr. Hall said that from the evidence of a ballistics expert it was obvious that the rifle had been held in one hand, probably by the wooden stock at the point of balance, and it was reasonable to assume that it had been held at the side of the body at the full extent of her arm.

Had there been any deliberate attempt to aim, the weapon would have been held either to the shoulder or at waist level.

'INCONSISTENT'

Medical evidence about the path of the bullet indicated that it had taken an upward direction in striking Gibbons, indicating that the rifle was much lower than the point of entry and supporting the defence claim that it was held below waist level.

Taken in all, this evidence was inconsistent with the deliberate firing of the rifle with intent to kill, Mr. Hall said.

He invited the jury to discover any intention from the opinion of the psychiatric expert.

There were five fields: Police evidence, independent witnesses, the statement by the accused to the police, the statement by the accused read in court and the expert evidence of Dr. Simpson.

Mr. Hall said there were indications of bias against the accused in the police evidence.

"Two witnesses had a partisan interest in having the girl convicted," he said.

Both Mr. Fenton and Miss Godfrey had a tendency to notice and somewhat exaggerate points which told against the girl to establish her guilt, and not to remember things which might have helped her defence.

'GILDED LILY'

"In fact, they gilded the lily," Mr. Hall said.

There were two occasions when they withheld evidence deliberately.

First was the remarkable failure by Miss Godfrey to remember the previous trouble at the house.

"Do you think she was being perfectly honest?" he asked the jury.

"You are entitled to infer that that was the incident referred to in the accused's statement when she was beaten with a billet of wood and ran away."

Miss Godfrey did not want this to go to the jury, and it was most reprehensible. Police

officers should not colour their evidence or hold back matter of this nature.

"Then the matter of the girl's demeanour, appearance and behaviour. Both officers said she appeared normal, yet first Mrs. Then Mr. Burgess clearly described her as a girl who was at least not herself in some respects. Mr. Burgess said she was in some kind of shock, and Mrs. Burgess said she had a grey face and rigid stance.

"But according to the police she was not in any peculiar condition of that kind, rather she was confident and self-assured even cheeky.

"And don't forget that Mr. Colquhoun said her voice was very quiet – not consistent with the picture of the cheeky girl police would have you believe she was."

Mr. Hall said that one thing the police witnesses agreed upon was that the girl showed no emotion.

It was quite possible that they had realized that lack of emotion may have been in her favour – as the defence contended on Dr. Simpson's evidence – it may have emerged before the jury in a different form.

There should have been some recognition given to the fact that a young girl who had seen her father fall down from a shot fired from a rifle she had been holding might need the opportunity to collect her wits and seek advice, but a hasty interview was conducted without any such recognition, although it was common procedure even in minor cases.

Although both officers knew it was desirable to have parent or some person present at such a time no action was taken to get someone.

'SUSPICIOUS'

"The police wanted to tie up this case against the girl and went out of their way to do it.

"You are entitled to regard their evidence with the highest suspicion," Mr. Hall told the jury.

He said the second occasion when evidence was withheld was when Det. Fenton denied in court that he had agreed to Dr. Simpson's suggestion that the accused's behaviour seemed automatic.

"This was when he realized that such an admission could weaken the Crown case," he added.

Mr. Hall claimed that when the girl got the rifle and loaded it she was not under the control of her normal will, but acting under a state of automatism. Dr. Simpson had been in the witness box a considerable time and had undergone a searching cross-

examination, but had maintained this conviction.

The trial is not expected to end before Monday afternoon.

EXAMINER newspaper Tuesday November 19th 1963

TEENAGER NEARS END

The trial of a 17-year-old girl charged with the attempted murder of her father at Launceston on July 6, will end today.

Shirley Ann Gibbons, of Lanoma St., Launceston, has pleaded not guilty to a charge of attempting to murder her father, Cyril Edward Gibbons and to an alternative charge of committing an act intended to cause grievous bodily harm.

The trial will enter its fifth day today, when Mr. Justice Crawford will sum up.

In the concluding stages of Mr. R. G. Hall's address to the jury yesterday morning, he said that according to police, Miss Gibbons had been quite anxious to tell the story of the alleged shooting.

"It is strange that she did not tell the full story. It shows that she was not mistress of herself in the normal way. She was not in full control of her faculties," he said.

He added that the girl's statement to police was not an attempt at justification of what she had done, but a dramatic fancy.

"CRISIS IN EMOTIONS"

"Think how the actions of a bully on a small child would affect her – she had said in her statement that she had seen and had been a victim of bullying," Mr. Hall said.

"The defence is not of provocation or justification, but these things have been put to you to show the cause of the crisis in her emotions on the day of the alleged offence."

Mr. Hall said the real question to be decided by the jury was intention.

"Taking the Crown evidence at its face value, you will find it impossible to be satisfied beyond a reasonable doubt that the 'action' was intentional," Mr. Hall said.

The Crown Prosecutor (Mr. J. B. Hutchins) said that Dr. Simpson, a Launceston psychiatrist, had allowed himself to depart from his own convictions – unconsciously perhaps – and fallen into the trap of siding too much with the defence.

Mr. Hutchins said the topics to which he pointed for support were:

. Dr. Simpson had acted in co-operation with Mr. Hall for some time – he had seen a draft of the unsworn statement by the girl and had seen fit to relay to Mr. Hall his interpretation of a conversation he had with Det. Fenton on Tuesday afternoon;

. Dr. Simpson had perhaps retracted from the position of a true expert in the court to assist the jury as to the girl's state of mind at the relative time.

Mr. Hutchins said the definition of automatism had been varied by Dr. Simpson, who had added to the definition, "with a patchy recollection."

Mr. Hutchins referred to definitions from law reports from New Zealand and England:

."Automatism strictly means action without conscious volition – action which denoted conduct of which the doer is not conscious";

. "Doing something without knowledge of it, and without remembering afterwards having done it";

. "Action without any knowledge of acting."

He said that these reasons were why he said Dr. Simpson's definition was not a true definition of automatism at all.

Mr. Hutchins said that a charge of attempted murder was almost the most difficult crime to prove, because it must be proved that there was an intention to kill the victim.

He said that there were certain facts in the case which could not be erased; therefore, the defence had endeavoured to get around them with the suggestion of amnesia.

Mr. Hutchins told the jury: "If the girl told Dr. Simpson that she could not remember certain things, why didn't she tell the police?"

"She knew well what she was doing at the time.

"A blackout is one of the first ways out for a guilty conscience and one of the most popular defences."

Mr. Justice Crawford said the case was a difficult one, particularly concerning the question of mental ingredients.

"I think the girl has become critical because of her life – critical of her family and critical of her interrogators," he said.

Mr. Justice Crawford said the notes made by Policewoman Sen.-Const. W. Godfrey appeared to fit in "pretty well with the evidence given by Det. Fenton."

GIRL'S STATEMENT

"I would also think that the girl's statement to the police "Does a person need any specific reason other than hate, loathing, disgust, for removing something that has done no good whatever in his lifetime and is never likely to?' was an attempt at justification for her action.

"The doctor says she showed no attempt at self-preservation – I would think the attempt at justification was an attempt at self-preservation."

The statement had also shown a critical attitude. The statement, "There's nothing much else I can say except that I am glad I had the courage to do it" surely showed intention, His Honour said.

He said it seemed almost impossible that her statement to the police was not a true account of the facts.

Mr. Justice Crawford said there had been no explanation as to accidental discharge except that the girl had said in her unsworn statement that she might have accidentally hit the trigger.

The trial is adjourned until 9.45.a.m. today.

EXAMINER newspaper Wednesday November 20th 1963

GIRL FREED OF SHOOTING

A Launceston Supreme Court jury yesterday acquitted a 17-year-old girl of a charge of attempting to murder her father at Launceston on July 6.

The jury also returned a verdict of not guilty on an alternative count of committing an act intended to cause grievous bodily harm to her father, Cyril Edward Gibbons.

The girl, Shirley Ann Gibbons, of Lanoma St., Launceston, had pleaded not guilty. Her trial lasted four and a half days.

Miss Gibbons showed little emotion in the dock as the jury foreman announced the

verdicts, but was joyfully reunited with her mother outside the court.

She briefly closed her eyes in the dock and lowered her head, but otherwise showed no signs of emotion.

Her mother, who was sitting in the back of the public gallery yesterday morning, occasionally showed obvious distress.

There were eight women among the gallery of about 30 people.

In his final summing up to the jury yesterday morning, Mr. Justice Crawford said that, leaving Dr. Simpson's evidence out, there could not be a stronger case of deliberate shooting.

However, Dr. Simpson's evidence stood uncontradicted.

"Normally, if there is no reason to doubt that he is partisan or that his evidence falls down in itself, there is no reason why you should not accept his evidence.. If it raises a reasonable doubt in your minds about her state of mind at the time, you should acquit the girl," His Honour told the jury.

"I see no reason why you should not accept Dr. Simpson's evidence," he said.

The jury retired at 10.35 and returned their verdict at 11.35 a.m.

Mr. J. B. Hutchins prosecuted for the Crown, and Mr. R. G. Hall appeared for Miss Gibbons.

Miss Gibbons was unavailable for comment at the end of proceedings. It is believed she has no definite plans for the future.

She eluded a small crowd of people waiting at the entrance of the Supreme Court by leaving through a rear entrance.

Mr. Hall said she was "very distressed."

{Articles courtesy of the Examiner newspaper}

8. Vienna, Budapest, Transylvania and Bangkok – the blogs

2010: Hobart Tasmania

Pre-Blog! Leaving 4 March for the erstwhile Austro-Hungarian Empire!

Transylvania – is that really a place?

This is the response I most often receive when I say that is where we are going for our holidays this year. The next question is inevitably "So where exactly is it?" In short, Transylvania is a real place and is in Romania. For a thousand years, up until WW1, it was part of Hungary. In the 10thC a Hungarian tribe called the Székely, settled in what it called Erdély ('beyond the forest' – the literal meaning of Transylvania).

It is a quite large region bordered by the Carpathian mountains about 100,000 square kilometres (Tasmania is 68,000 square kilometres so about two thirds of the size) and is most well known, infamously, as the mythic home of Count Dracula.

The dark side

Bram Stoker's book about Count Dracula had some basis in historical fact. In the 15thC a local ruler by the name of Vlad Tepes engaged in brutal reprisals against enemies both real and imagined including impaling whole villages on stakes and leaving them to die in the most horrendous circumstances. He was known as The Devil or "Dracul" (in Romanian) and Bram Stoker used this "nickname"" for his character. In the 16thC there was a Countess Elizabeth Bathory who favoured the blood of dead virgins as her bath of choice. In that sense she was rather more akin to Bram's character than Vlad Tepes. Transylvania's own mythic creature of choice is actually the werewolf or the shape-shifting spirit. Priculici are spirits of the dead who can turn themselves into animals. Moroi are the spirits of unbaptised babies who turn into haunters of their mothers (a catholic tale to be sure). Strigoi are demons who inhabit the bodies of the dead or generally the troubled souls of the dead who can also turn into animals – wolves or perhaps bats. So again Bram Stoker (who never visited Transylvania) utilised some of these myths and legends to help create his composite character. Nicolai Ceausescu was arguably the 20Cth version of this character.

And we are going there because.....

My mother was a Szekely from a village called Miklósvár (Miclosoara in Romanian) near the Eastern Carpathians. The Szekely remained a distinct grouping within Hungary rather like the highlanders in Scotland consider themselves part of yet different from other Scots. Many stories exist as to their origins. Some say Scythian. My mother was in agreement with the view held primarily within the Szekely community that they were descended from the seven sons of Attila the Hun. The Szekely are certainly considered to be some of the finest warriors to have ever existed. There are still over 600,000 Szekely in Romania although Ceausescu had a plan to bulldoze all the Hungarian villages. Thankfully he was strung up before this plan took effect.

Her family left the home they had lived in for 400 years (no, they were not undead) in 1927 when my mother was seven years old. Most Hungarian gentry were squeezed or forced to leave their properties in the decade after WW1. My mother's family moved to another town in Transylvania before finally relocating to Budapest in the late 1930s. For the whole of my mother's life she mourned leaving her Miklósvár – even though she was only seven years old when she left. Some of her memories were vivid although primarily, I speculate, because they had been continually reinforced and to some extent created for her by her own mother who died at the ripe old age of 90 in 1982.

My mother's links with Transylvania were slim and frail and the only news she ever heard about their former house was that, at some stage, it had been destroyed, probably in a fire. The former house was described as a large keep or fortress of some kind although such terms are probably used as loosely as 'castle' in Transylvania. She remembers picking wild raspberries as a toddler and looking up to see a bear eating raspberries on the other side of the bushes. This memory is arguably distinctly her own. During her life we were never able to find a map which showed Miklósvár and we were never able to find any references to Miklósvár on the internet. So it became a place of myth for me as well as for her.

After she died in 2007 strangely (and tragically) references to Miklósvár started to pop up on the computer. The main reference was to a Count Tibor Kalnoky who had seemingly reclaimed his family's hunting manor in Miklósvár and restored a number of local cottages as guesthouses. He has turned it into a thriving business. My first thought was that the Count was an imposter and a usurper and that, in fact, he had taken my mother's home as his own. Subsequent information has led to some uncertainty as (a) my mother's home supposedly destroyed and (b) sources in Romania say that there were indeed other 'large houses' in Miklósvár.

Mysteries to be unravelled and fun to be had

The first mystery is to actually find the ruins of my mother's home or to confront the Count!

The second mystery is to find out why there are at least 30 people listed in the local telephone directory for Miklósvár with my mother's maiden surname. Not to cast any aspersions on my mother but if they were an important family in Miklósvár then why do they have lots of poor cousins? Brushing up on Hungarian as we speak!

We will also provide a definitive answer as to the origin of the Szekely!!

Most importantly, this is my last chance to be 'with' my mother. I will be living in her shoes, in her memories, in her heart. She will be with me and I will be seeing the world that she saw through her childhood eyes. It will be my chance to lovingly say goodbye to her in a final glorious sweep through a lost past.

We also would hope to have a really great time visiting this remote and rather mysterious part of the world. Reputedly Transylvania contains half of all the remaining wolves in Europe which does rather indicate a medieval state of industrial development although Ceausescu did his best to try to overturn this. He and his cronies hunted with machine guns. Not very sporting. Have prebooked everything including a car and a driver so that we can be carefree tourists with no need to translate No Parking signs from Romanian and so we can escape from restaurants without having inadvertently ordered pigs' ears in lard as a main course.

That's the preamble and the background finished. Before we get to Transylvania we spend a few days in Vienna and a week in Budapest.

2010: Vienna

"Dear Family and Friends

Vienna

The world tilted slightly on its axis at this, the beginning of the latest travel spectacular. Not too much of a disaster in relation to, say, terrorism or world poverty, but the small world of the traveller reacts extremely badly to each incident designed to put a spoke in its wheel. Kate suffered from a seat which would not recline ALL the way from Melbourne to Dubai. 15 hours sitting bolt upright is a significantly

217

worse proposition than sitting 15 hours with the ability to sit slightly less than bolt upright and that's bad enough in Scumbag Class seats. Repeated appeals to Emirates staff resulted in (a) being looked straight through and (b) a male passenger being upgraded to Business Class in front of our very eyes so that Kate could be moved to an alternative Scumbag Class seat about 3 kilometres away from Shirley. This was rejected as being an equally unsatisfactory solution and we desisted from further pressure as we decided that we simply couldn't bear to see any more male passengers upgraded to solve our 'problem'. We grinned and beared it.

Had a reasonably ok stopover in Dubai after we spent a goodly hour or two actually finding the Dubai International Airport Hotel inside the vast terminal building. "Under no circumstances must transit passengers exit the terminal building" OR "They will NOT be allowed back in until 3 hours before their flight departure". We asked many a likely and unlikely looking person about the whereabouts of the elusive hotel (would it really kill them to put up a few signs??) and were told variously to go up to the next level or to go back down to the next level. Finally found ourselves in deep consultation with a non-English speaking cleaner somewhere in the bowels of the terminal who insisted that we needed to go through doors which led to THE OUTSIDE of the Terminal building and re-enter across the other side. As we had completely run out of options we hesitantly did this, to be confronted immediately by an officious official who.... did not lock us out but proved to be Helpful. That was a close one. Rested like mad until it was time to catch the final leg to Vienna. Actually had quite a decent room service meal which we ate without wine as the wine offering was "House wine – red, white or blush - $70 a bottle". Dedicated wine drinkers that we are we baulked at this.

Vienna flight was nice and we reclined at will. Even the Emirates staff were more pleasant –

more women than men. The Viennese on the plane attempted a mad rush to exit when we landed as if they had all been deprived for far too long of cake and cream.

However on arrival the most ghastly axis tilting event of the traveller – LOST LUGGAGE (Shirley's). Given that we had come from 35 degrees and were about to resurface in Vienna (forecast maximum 1 degree) and a small backpack did not hold out much possibility for extra layers this was highly unpleasant. Not to mention the camera, the laptop, the underwear (!), the sponge bag, the train tickets to Budapest, all our travel books and lots of itinerary stuff, the Metamucil (!), the spare shoes aaarrghhhhh......

Emirates staff were strangely absent from any of the post luggageless procedures. Austrian Airlines acted as their benighted agent and were remarkably helpful ("No, sadly Emirates do not provide you with any funding for emergency supplies but do keep receipts as they MIGHT reimburse you at some later stage") and ("Oh look here is an emergency bathroom supply kit which you can have from Emirates – oh no it's for men, bad luck there"). With hindsight we should have been able to predict that last one.

We've decided to wear burkas if we ever do travel Emirates again (which we absolutely definitely and for ever will not) as this is the only possible appropriate way to acknowledge that, yes, women are crap.

So, Vienna. Well indeed it was 1 degree but also actually snowing. But we had to go out, Shirley in filthy tattered shirt sleeves, to buy at the very least some underwear. Whilst out we also had a go at a Viennese coffee shop which produced worse coffee than Geeveston and that was the baddest coffee we had ever had previously. Have to figure out what exactly we should be ordering as we clearly don't have the hang of it. Underwear shopping was achieved and then, adventuresome pair that we are, we decided to eat at the hotel and have an early night. Well for goodness sake we were depressed, it was snowing outside, Kate was still getting over all that upright sitting, Shirley had no clothes and......the leopard doesn't change its spots all that much even when travelling.

Next day after a splendid breakfast (had all three – the Australian, the English and the European) did a self guided tour of the Old Town which ceased abruptly after Shirley's teeth nearly chattered out of her head and she decided that she was developing severe frostbite in all ten fingers. So went into the warmth of the Jewish Museum and then home for lunch!! Might not manage to eat anywhere except the hotel for our entire stay. Anyway it has a lovely thing called a Business Lounge which we have claimed as our own (can drink, eat AND smoke).

Joy of joys – luggage has turned up – much blogging to be done forthwith.

All for now. Much happier.

Love from Shirley and Kate"

2010: Vienna and Budapest

"Dear Family and Friends

Vienna to Budapest

We won't whine quite as much in this one!

Yesterday we wended our way around more bits of Wien. Goodness me but Vienna really gets its kicks from grand grand buildings all of which start to merge together by the end of the day. We donned many layers (Shirley very pleased to have many layers to don) and set off into the extremely chilly morning. A definite highlight was the visit to the Hotel Sacher to sample the famous torte. We were in complete agreement that the cream was an inferior example of its kind and that the torte was a little dry and that

Shirley's sachertorte is BETTER. Will have a cake afternoon on return using grandma's secret recipe. However the man in the cloakroom was very nice and told us an incomprehensible joke about two rabbis. We felt obliged to return the favour and told him the 'One one was a race horse' ditty. He found this equally incomprehensible. Then found the market – art nouveau buildings quite nice – altogether too damn cold though. Via many other big huge grand buildings including the RatHaus, we shivered our way back home for yet another in-house lunch. Firmly decided that we had better eat somewhere other than the hotel at least once so sampled an Indian restaurant round the corner which was adequate.

Up to catch the train to Budapest. Lovely trip – really, trains are the only civilised way to travel – pity there aren't any in Tasmania. Changed Euros into Forints (F1,000 = EU4!!). Budapest is a beautiful city and, though tired, we felt compelled to go for a rather long walk. It turns out that we accidentally achieved one of the recommended walks so can cross that off the list. Plans for this evening include eating bread and cheese in our quite large apartment and watching the final episode of Durham County on ABC IView – dontcha just love the ABC.

Well now we hate the ABC – turns out you can't watch IView unless you are in Australia damn it.

Did Castle Hill today – the medieval old town which is superior to Stockholm's old town – the hitherto favourite. Really lovely. Castle Hill also includes the famous folly, the Fishermen's Bastion which gives fabulous views over the Danube. Many museums and galleries so we decided we had better go to at least one. Chose the Budapest History Museum which turned out to be full of bits of ancient underground castles excavated right there on the spot and heavily armed guards – in case you ran off, puffing, with a bit of old wall. Eschewed the odd little tourist trap such as the funicular thingy which runs up and down to Castle Hill and walked back to our hotel across the Chain Bridge. Oh, and had goulash for lunch as opposed to Szendvics (sandwiches we assume) which kept the cold out for at least four minutes. We are very happy to be here. Apart, that is, from the fact that the only bottle of Hungarian wine we've had so far tasted like Murray Cod. Pizza for dinner with a bottle of ITALIAN wine. Ho hum. We both have prolifically bleeding noses – from the extreme cold rather than from any cocaine addictions which might have been suddenly acquired.

Went on the first of our pre-organised tours today, to Hapsburg Franz Joseph and Elizabeth (Sisi) palace at Godollo, (with an umlaut on every single O), approximately 30kms from Budapest. Bit of a relief at first as it was snowing heavily and we had less than no inclination to go out anywhere. However our tour guide turned out to be a virulent racist and it became quite uncomfortable, especially knowing that we have her again for 10 hours on Saturday.

Do you speak, do you keep quiet, aaarrggh. Did have some good goss though as in Franz had syphilis and gonorrhea so they both had black teeth after the treatment of the day which was mercury. Franz Joseph had many "mattresses" apparently – we later worked out that this was supposed to be "mistresses" – but same thing really. Anyway not a lot of smiling in ye olde court portraits and photos cos of the teeth thing. The palace was gorgeous, especially so in the snow. Apparently we had paid for cake as part of the package so were forced to pick at a large choccy number even though what we really wanted was a toasted ham, cheese and tomato szendvic. Back home and immediately popped out for selfsame szendvic which we actually found – fresh mozzarella, prosciutto and tom being the local very acceptable version.

Shirley not very well – dunno what that's about but she's not sparking on all cylinders so we had a quiet arvo – no option really given the heavily iced precipitation – then went next door, literally, to yet another Indian restaurant. We decided to order quite modestly, bearing in mind Shirley not feeling well and a reasonably recent szendvic consumption which turned out to be very wise as the portions were Chicago style HUGE. Eg 4 samosas in one entree serve. Still love Budapest but would pay a king's ransom for an extra degree or two in the temperature.

Did a Shirley "mother" day today which involved 3 metro trips, 4 bus trips and one tram trip. First up to the Farkas Temeti (literal translation = Wolf Cemetery) which is where her family's house was after they moved to Budapest (not actually IN the cemetery). Not there of course as it was bombed during WW11 but got a general idea of the area. SFBCaS (Still Freezing Bloody Cold and Snowing).

Then to the Citadel on Gellert Hill which had a display of photos from the Siege of Budapest in 44-45. The display was in a cold, damp, ghastly concrete bunker and further chilled us with its dreadful photos. My mother was bombed whilst in a bomb shelter and lay there in the cold and snow for 10 days before being dug out by the Russians. When they emerged the area was a hotspot of street to street fighting and she had to run on a broken ankle through a hail of bullets.......my grandmother ran BACK to the shelter because she had forgotten the chocolate which had kept them alive – along with snow melt water. We feel that we got some very faint idea of what it must have been like – a living, breathing hell of cold, fear, bombs, degradation and starvation.

This took us the whole day mainly because whilst we mastered very quickly the art of getting ON buses it took a little longer to work out how to get OFF them.

Had lunch at a hotel on Gellert hill which consisted of an entree each which could have kept a small family alive for a week.

Today we met up with our racist tour guide and went to Lake Balaton and the Herend factory. The Herend factory was a major success, extremely well organised, beautiful museum, gift shop, restaurant and mini-manufactory demonstrations. Our favourite was a large espresso coffee machine in the Victoria pattern which cost 4,200,000 Forints (a steal at about $16,000).

A walking tour of the old town in Veszprem was not such a success as our gaily bleeding noses indicated that the biting wind had lowered the temperature to about -10 degrees. Thence to the Tihanyi peninsula on Lake Balaton where we wanted to buy a house and settle down forever – reed thatched roofs, cobbled streets reminiscent of small villages in England and, according to our tour guide, largely owned by the British! Altogether a successful day – Kate even tasted the health giving mineral waters. We won't say what we had for dinner.

As we have rather taken to our racist tour guide (Helen) we are joining up with her again today for a walking tour of the Jewish quarter (suppose she will have to curb her racism somewhat....) It is forecast to be a balmy 6 degrees so we may fling some of our outer layers off in anticipation.

And we did so fling but quickly flung them on again. Highlight of the tour was the Holocaust Museum which was conducted as a separate mini-tour by an in-house guide and was extremely moving. We decided not to continue with Helen as she would have tainted the commentary of this experience and skived off to Gerbaud which is the Budapest version of the Sacher Hotel. Quite beautiful, reasonable lunch, crap coffee (the first bad coffee we have had here). However a landmark not to be missed – last time Shirley was in Budapest 40 years ago she failed to even FIND Gerbaud much to her mother's complete disgust. Shirley's quite real excuse was that streets were frequently blocked by Communist parades......

Then on to a sort of Metro tour of Budapest. We are very impressed by the Metro – have not had to wait more than about 30 seconds for a train no matter how obscure our route. Main destination, apart from Kate's frequent side trips to view amazing Art Nouveau buildings, was the Ethnographic Museum. This did indeed house some great ethnographic exhibitions, the most significant of which was a detailed study of a traditional Hungarian village in the 1950's before Communism disappeared it. Detailed down to the number and type of hoes possessed by each individual family – strangely compelling. Included were the actual hoes. Because Communism did disappear it. However we will find present day working examples of its kind when we get to Transylvania. Kate is being very brave in the face of the increasing strangeness of everything. Thank goodness she has *some* acquaintance with all this....otherwise she would have jacked up and gone to the Greek Islands by now.

Won't tell you what we had for dinner.

Tomorrow is Hungarian National Day.

Hungarian National Day: Those of you who were 'with us' in Venice will remember that we had amazing difficulties getting any info about the Festival of Salute (nothing on websites, no posters, blank looks from everyone we asked), well the same seems to be true of Hungarian National Day on Monday 15 March. We first became alerted to this when we overheard some people asking about it at the hotel reception desk. They were firmly told "Oh that is just for Hungarians". We then asked our racist tour guide and she said "Yes yes many things happening – marches, speeches, meetings." When further pressed she said "Parliament house – ask your reception desk to print out the website". We searched endlessly for websites but with little result. If we found anything at all it was general in the extreme. Gulp, we will have to pretend that we are Hungarians and ask at the reception desk. Not holding our breaths.

Shirley spent a goodly amount of time with an on-line dictionary and managed to find the words for National, Day, Parade, Military, Horse and the like and regurgitated all this at the front desk. Well, it seemed to do the trick and we are in possession of Most Secret Information about the many events to be held tomorrow. We are hoping for hussars on horseback and do believe there is a strong chance of this.

Last day in Budapest.

Using our Most Secret Information we found many sites where celebrations were happening but got to each of them just as hussars on horsebacks' bottoms were moving away or were in the process of dismounting. Entertainment, aside from the dismounting hussars, was a little on the spare side – the occasional speech, the occasional military band wearing recycled soviet uniforms, pretzels and cardboard hussar hats seemed to be it – so we have scuttled to the warmth of our hotel room to pack for TRANSYLVANIA.

Also tracked down the Shoes on the Danube sculpture. About 50 pairs of scattered shoes in memory of the many Hungarian Jews who were thrown into the freezing river by the Nazi Hungarian Arrow Cross Party. Really poignant and felt as though it had happened 5 minutes ago.

Popped a couple of photos in this blog – if that is a problem for anyone's email let us know. Viszlat for now. Must learn how to say hello and thank you in Romanian before tomorrow."

Transylvania 1

Picked up at our hotel in Budapest by man in shiny black mercedes who drove us lickety split to Transylvania. Well it was lickety split on motorways until we reached Romania and then it was crawl, dodge potholes, keep an eye on maniacal Romanian drivers (all of them are maniacal - "Romanians routinely risk death just to gain 3 seconds on their journeys, even if they are just going to church" Lonely Planet Guide) and maintain an average speed of about 30km an hour. Arrived in Timisoara at about lunchtime. Immediately met by our next driver/tour guide in his BMW who will be with us for the next three weeks. Istvan initially made contact with us via Facebook while we were in Budapest! We think of ourselves as being carried around in a modern day version of Jane Franklin's sedan chair. He took us for a quickish tour of downtown which we managed to turn into a homely little shopping trip (moisturiser, soap, change money etc).

"Timisoara (Hungarian:*Temesvar*) population about 320,000

4rth largest city in Transylvania is dubbed the city of flowers after the ring of pretty parks that surround it. It is the most developed city and the richest agricultural area. In the heart of the old town is Timisoara's most picturesque square "union square" because of the imposing sight of the Catholic and Serbian churches facing each other. This is where the overthrow of Ceausescu really got a head of steam". – source Lonely Planet Guide

The reality is that this place is an enormous shock – generally large buildings between 3 and 8 stories, some communist era and some Hapsburg era and even much much older. ALL without exception looking like peeling, rusting, filthy leftovers from a Noir version of a Harry Potter film. Scary weird shapes (the really old buildings) and lurching, leaning concrete catastrophes draped with laundry and well, dirt (the newer buildings). The view from our hotel window is of ghastly rubbish strewn backyards and general detritus. The hotel is nice and, as such, quite out of place. It is supposed to be in the centre of something but we are not sure what. You can really see why this place (and other poor Eastern European countries) is such a target for the traffickers in women – white slave traders. In fact the whole place looks as though it could be sold off in a mortgagee sale for very little money. Apparently this city was once beautiful – known as 'little Vienna'. Guess Communism and the GFC did it no favours. However it is also fascinatingly strange and different and we think we will thoroughly have experiences that could not be had anywhere else (both good and bad) in Transylvania. Went out with Istvan for a Romanian meal – very cheap, very good, but we have to find a polite way to be by ourselves in the evenings – so we can have a thorough and critical debrief! Discovered that our hotel not quite so good after all - power points don't work, shower floods all over the floor, a remarkable and chronic shortage of toilet paper (when we asked for more were given the teeniest little roll containing about 12 sheets...). Do believe that within a year or two the hotel will be swallowed up into the general decay and miasma of its surroundings. Dog barked all night but managed to listen to Radio National ABC via internet streaming. Aaah home!

This morning, after oversleeping and very odd breakfast which included goat butter, faced bright sunshine which was actually somewhat warm and managed to have a simply wonderful day. Got in our sedan chair and transported to wander around amid once gorgeous turreted decaying Gaudi inspired buildings, dodging bits of crumbling masonry (shades of the palazzo in San Marco!), had hamburger with chips INSIDE the burger for lunch and visited three museums. Actually only two because we think one of them might have been closed – or open, who knows. The ones that we got into were sort of partially open. Thank goodness for our guide who managed to find women with buckets who sold entry tickets standing in unlikely places after going up and down stairs and round corners and along corridors and seeing most of the exhibits before paying. Won't bore you with the details but all probably interesting though only signed in Romanian so not at all sure what we saw. Made our guide take us to see some slightly less touristy areas which were, or once had been, equally as magnificent as all the rest. We want to wrap this city up and restore it piece by piece, it was so obviously glorious about for so many centuries and is now wrecked beyond belief.

Will not debrief in quite so much detail at all our stops as we are sure that the story will be similar no matter where we are in Transylvania. The long and short of it is that most of the terrific stuff was all built during the last 1,000 years and that the Communists destroyed or allowed to be destroyed everything that wasn't Communist. This was followed immediately by 'Romanianisation' which has done much the same. They will only value and maintain stuff which relates to their 'Roman' past and given that that consists only and entirely of a few ancient relics from 2,000 years ago there will not be much left here after another 50 years or so.

"**Arad (*Arad*)**

Situated in lush wine making country on the banks of the Mures River and boasts elegant 19thC architecture. Lies at the edge of the Carpathian Mountains in the centre of the Crisana region. Elegant architecture." – Lonely Planet

Set off for Arad at 9 in our, by now, rather cramped, sedan chair and had been happily travelling along an increasingly rutted road for an hour, with our driver becoming quieter and quieter, when Kate got out our very large map of Transylvania to see exactly where we were. A look of some relief on the driver's face who grabbed the map and announced that we were actually nowhere and would need to retrace our route back to Temesvar. His GPS had failed him yet again and he doesn't carry any maps! So we lost two hours which enabled only a quick stop in Arad so no opinions formed except that the toilets in McDonalds are very clean.

Thence to Oradea although GPS failure meant that we took a very long time to find our hotel. By now just a little bit crabby.

"Oradea (*Nagyvarad*)

One of the most imposing sights is the Orthodox Moon Church which has an unusual lunar mechanism on its tower that changes position in accordance with the moon's movements. An air of arresting but faded grandeur" – Lonely Planet.

Arresting but faded grandeur could be iterated for most of the Transylvania we have seen so far! Our hotel was complete rubbish though in a good location so we shook off our tour guide and wandered around by ourselves. The main reason we came here was to "find" my grandparent's vineyard! We didn't have any hope of this but got a nice feel for the place. Had a moderately OK meal, mainly consisting of chips, in the hotel dining room.

Even crabbier the next day after a sleepless night (yowling cats, claustrophobic bedroom, shower which completely fell to bits) set off across the snow covered Apuseni Mountains for next stop, Cluj-Napoca. Our tour guide has definitely NOT approved of any of our destinations so far – "not good tourist spots – nothing to see" – we beg to differ as we have been completely entranced and mesmerised by everything we are seeing. This was a great trip and included a whole village completely consisting of gypsy owned houses, nearly all of them unlived in. They are huge and have ornate stainless steel roofs to shine in the sun with various symbols carved into them, such as Ferrari, Mercedes Benz or Euro!!

Arrived at our hotel (GPS failure again), decided the room was too small and not about to put up with that again so upgraded ourselves to the VIP suite for the princely sum of about an extra $15 – major relief.

"Cluj Napoca (*Kolozsvar*)

Cluj is largely a university town with trendy bars, shops and cafes." – You know who.

Went to Ethnographic Museum (will probably do this everywhere!) which was really good although as with all museums we have visited so far, we were the only visitors. At least 10 staff watched us closely and kept turning lights off a bit quick. In fact, we have been the only tourists we have seen in the whole of Transylvania so far...... Bought Romanian wine at a very exclusive wine shop where we were sorely tempted to buy the Australian wine they had on offer but resisted.

So, although we dropped our bundles a bit yesterday have picked them up again remarkably well. Really an extraordinary trip – you just have to figure out how to look after yourselves (eg upgrade to VIP suite).

Oh and BTW 13 degrees, sun shining, Kate in shirtsleeves.

Probably need to send this off now before it gets too long. You won't be quizzed on the content – it is as detailed as WE want it!!

Photos are of view from hotel window in Temesvar, Gaudi inspired house in Temesvar and smoko with ox cart on route to Cluj.

Lots of love from Shirley and Kate

Dear Everyone

Transylvania 2

Hotel room and Toilet report

Bad toilet day today! Stopped at a small glass icon museum in a very small village. Indoor toilet was not working so we were directed to a 'long drop' toilet round the back which we both decided we would use only after we had a lobotomy – if then. Istvan asked our very good tour guide to speed up the commentary which she did and then we sped to the nearest petrol station which proved to be the inside version of the 'long drop'. Lesson: don't drink so much water when on the road!

Have managed to destroy two hotel rooms so far. Kate ripped the whole shower assembly off the wall in Oradea and then proceeded to do much the same thing in the hotel in Cluj-Napoca as well as ripping the curtains down. Istvan suggested we do it properly next time and throw the TV out the window. Hmm.

Diatribes: Shirley keen on channeling her mother and spouting diatribes against the Romanians (fot taking Transylvania off the Hungarians and then for ruining it..) however this means that Kate responds rationally and calmly and accuses Shirley of being a bit of a racist. Shirley has discovered however that if she holds her tongue, Kate will spontaneously take over the diatribes and all's well with the world.

Got back in our sedan chair sardine can (yes it seems to get smaller every day and we've hardly bought anything)... and set off for the Turda Gorge (just before you reach 'Cunta' if you may need directions at some time). Kate and Istvan did the walky thing down the track while Shirley hung around at base station guarding the sedan chair. She is really very lazy and doesn't seem to mind a bit. Anything with a potential UP bit to it will get thumbs down from her. Which reminds us of the taxi Shirley made us get in Kolozsvar in order to go back UP to our hotel – it cost about $1.50. Prices for everything are incredibly cheap. Room service dinner last night (pizza and salad) cost $7 – yes $7!!!!!

"Alba Ulia (*Gyulaferhervar*)

Has an imposing Alba Carolina Citadel, richly carved with sculptures in the baroque style. One of the main streets runs up from the lower town to the first gate of the fortress, adorned with sculptures inspired by Greek mythology."

A really impressive huge fortress/citadel from the 11thC – we had bean and pork soup in the old armoury which was pleasantly touristy – but we were the only ones there. Then confronted Istvan and said NO MORE MUSEUMS unless we pick them so he took us instead to a fantastic old fortified Saxon church 13thC in a really really small village. It was tiny but hugely impressive as not run by the Romanian government (oops there I go again).

Thence to the glass icon museum of toilet fame and on to Sibiu. Becoming more spectacular and we can see the Fagaras Mountains in the distance (part of the Carpathians at last) which are immense, snow capped and make Shirley all teary eyed.

We are starting to speak English with a Romanian twist. For example, one of us actually said to Istvan, "we will make the meeting with you at 9 in the morning".

"Sibiu (*Nagyszeben*)

One of Transylvania's prettiest and most pleasant cities with its medieval fortress, Liar's Bridge and one of the best art galleries in Romania, the Bruckental Art Museum."

Great hotel, instant upgrade, evening stroll through Sibiu as it is really quite warm now.

Checked Tasmanian elections on internet – what a mess......

Sibiu is one of Transylvania's saxon towns/cities/villages – we are in the heart of Saxon heritage now and it is all impressive, particularly because it is all beautifully maintained and/or restored. We go 'ho hum' if anything is not at least 12thC. 16thC and 17thC leaves us quite cold. Had great meals both nights, in Small Square and Big Square (so neither one would feel left out) and then discovered that Istvan had royally dined on KFC both nights so we will never trust his gastronomic recommendations again. We walked quite close to the Bruckental Art Museum and took a picture of it but didn't manage to enter as it was just too lovely wandering around.

"Biertan (*Berethalom*)

World Heritage listed 15thC church in undeveloped lovely small village."

Actually another fortified Saxon church – double walls. You wouldn't have wanted to attack this place in a fit. We know that few people come to Transylvania but it has treasures beyond compare. And thence to one of our real highlight places......

"Sighisoara (*Segesvar*)

Preserved medieval citadel at its core and surrounded by beautiful hilly countryside". Described by Gavin Stamp as "Ghormanghast"

Oh and it is. Have run out of superlatives damn it! Our hotel is a medieval building right inside the citadel which has, of course, immense walls and nine remaining towers – the citadel that is. It is also, apart from being (add own superlatives here), very manageable which is a relief to the weary tourist. We had to climb many steps today (174 to the top of the covered staircase) but after that walked around the walls and the towers, dipping in to one of the churches which had 17thC persian rugs around the walls. Tempted but....

Visited the Old School at the top of the staircase (children are very fit here) and Shirley, under the mistaken impression that it was a Monument, flung the door open, to be confronted with sleepy children, all of whom immediately sprang to attention thinking the School Inspector had arrived. Shirley smacked one of them for slouching and we moved on, rather quickly. Couldn't get internet at our hotel which the staff blamed on Shirley's very small computer "If you had a bigger laptop you could get...."

"Targu Mures ((*Marosvasarhely*)

Orthodox Cathedral and the Palace of Culture, famous for its collection of glass painted icons and mirrors. Flamboyant Hapsburg architecture. Sizable Roma population."

A rather nasty city we thought, with no real heart but we weren't there very long AND had just come from Sighisoara so it couldn't really compare..... However we did go to the Palace of Culture to see the 19thC stained glass windows representing 12 different Szekely folk tales which were incredibly wonderful, slightly Disney-ish with gorgeous colours and very large to boot. Refused any more museums and came to Bistrita for the night. We think Istvan had a hangover today as he was a teeny bit grumpy but really who wouldn't be having to drag two old ladies' bags and persons all round the place for 3 weeks. And he is not allowed to tell any more jokes, and we refuse to eat dinner at 8.30! And his car/sedan chair really does get smaller all the time. What a chore for him. He really is doing a fabulous job of putting up with us.

"Bistrita (*Beszterce*)

A small market town trapped in the form of a city."

Quick scan of the menu in this hotel reveals such delicacies as 'cock's testicles' (a very small meal?), 'mutton at oven' (roast lamb? We live in hope) and 'boiled carp with boiled potatoes'. Might see if there is a pizzeria somewhere.

Oh and it's all becoming a bit more Dracula oriented which is a chore. However they are all equally as besotted with Prince Charles who is 'saving' bits of Transylvania (which is good) but we are nearly as bored with chat about him as we are with D.

Will send this off now as laptop might be too small to get internet at next hotel which is up in the mountains somewhere and they might not even know what the internet is.

Lots of love for now

Kate and Shirley

Dear very far off Friends and Family

The endlessly enchanting small villages which we pass through, usually very slowly because of horse drawn carriages and potholes, consist mainly of 2 or 3 room little houses (unless they are gypsy 'palaces' in which case they are gargantuan – yes we have absorbed the local racism), mostly dusty brown but occasionally painted a startling shade of daffodil yellow, sky blue, intense lime, bright orange or luminous cerise. Coincidentally Kate has a set of blouses in these exact same colours and has frequently surprised the population of entire Romanian cities by appearing before them dressed as a peasant house.

Our sedan chair now smells constantly of a perfidious mixture of garlic (lunches) and coconut (Istvan's air freshener).

For the very many of you who do not know really where we are and where we are going (which sometimes includes us) we will not be landing in Shirley's mother's village until Good Friday.

Speaking of Good Friday, all villagers (including school children) now seem to be engaged in very active spring cleaning in preparation for Easter – it will take them that long......

Summary of day: despite a 9am meeting with Istvan to formally demand a precise and manageable itinerary for the day (as he has a habit of jumping things on us) we ended up going to only one of the places we had insisted upon and five that were jumped on us, including a visit to a very fake concrete version of Dracula's castle. Not as bossy as we thought we were damn it.

"Tihuta – Campulung Moldivensc – Guru Humorului

Borgo Pass (Dracula's castle) – Wood Museum, Moldovita Monastery (UNESCO monument) and Bucovina Monasteries."

Had a wonderful drive across the 'small' Carpathian Mountains (about 1600 m high), much snow still on the ground and steep banks of conifers abounding. (The hills are alive with the sound of music). Borgo Pass was where Bram Stoker's Jonathan Harker supposedly crossed the mountains. Briskly cold, delightful and so very Transylvanian. Yes, went to the wood museum which had a nice 17thC wooden sleigh then to the first of our painted monasteries, Humor Monastery. They are painted all over on the inside AND the outside, gorgeous colours not too faded and still used as a monastery. The most angelic young nuns were sweeping the grass with old witches' brooms and were holy to behold. Thence to our fabulous lodgings, Hildes Residence, where we have, we assure you, no complaints at all. Bliss.

Lots and lots of painted Bucovina monasteries still to go – we may call a halt at some stage ....

Drank plum brandy last night, also forced to pop into the dining room at 9pm in dressing gown to deliver dirty knickers for washing as "the girl on duty next morning not to be trusted".

So, up and at it to view four more monasteries. This was after a very strange breakfast consisting initially of coffee (for drinking) and tea (for eating) - severe communication breakdown. According to the guidebook, one monastery is predominantly blue, one yellow, one pink and one red. To be henceforward known as the 'Wiggles monasteries'. We thought they were all predominantly blue, gold, yellow, red and pink and looked rather like someone who had had a complete body tattoo. But really quite unique, although exceptionally cold. The altars were almost heathen in their amazingly garish golden overwhelmingness (yes, large). One of the main monasteries we stopped at (Moldovita) possibly allegedly predominantly blue, was having its patron saint annual festival so we have an excellent movie of chanting monks but forgot to look at most of the stuff we were there to look at.

We are anxious each and every day about when we will stop for toilet/lunch/coffee or coffee/toilet/lunch or lunch/coffee/toilet depending on the time of day as to the order of importance. Today was no exception although we thought we had it under control until we got lost again (neither GPS or maps any help) and we found ourselves near the Ukrainian border to be rescued by a whining cow farmer.

Still had a great day as we whisked backwards and forwards across mountains and did end up having a nice little grilled trout for lunch plus alpine scenery.

"Targu Neamt (*Nemc*)

Ruins of a 14thC citadel, Bicaz Lake and Red Lake and Gheorghieni" – this is no longer from Lonely Planet but a crib from our so called itinerary.

Well you can't say that things in Transylvania aren't high. We skipped yet another ethnographic museum and asked Istvan to take us to our first non-church oriented citadel – an amazing fortress in the sky, stomach churning and beautiful, really well restored for a change. Then drove a bit quick across the High Carpathians trying not to look down at 2000m drops into icy, snowy, conifer covered wilderness. Bicaz Gorge was unlike anything we have ever imagined, sheer cliffs moving towards heaven and the Red Lake was completely frozen still – neither of us have ever seen a frozen lake before and were suitably gob smacked. Shirley cried (about the mountains which her mother so loved, not the Lake).

Arrive in Szekely Land (Shirley's mother's bit) to find, as known, that Ceausescu has done his worst – placed as many ghastly power schemes, factories etc as inhumanly possible in an attempt to rip the heart out of the place. Not totally successful and there remain little Hungarian villages with the wonderful carved Szekely gates and poles and many many proud Hungarians still. Usual fight with hotel about upgrading but successfully installed in a fabulous room with rocking chairs and balcony (dozy blowflies instantly squashed utilising hotel stationery). Pizza for dinner.

"Miercurea Ciuc (*Csikszereda*)

Over 80% Hungarian – the hub of Szekely Land. Miko Castle including the Szekely Museum of Csik and St Ana Lake"

A very drab city surrounded by wonderful mountains. Ceausescu ripped down ALL the buildings except for two and built factories and apartment blocks. One of the buildings left standing is Miko Castle which is quite out of place as very 16thC (but plain, not Hapsburgian) and houses what turned out to be a very disappointing Szekely Museum – weren't even allowed to SEE the main attraction which was their old Szekely gates as "the Museum Director has closed them". Decided against another lake (!) and went 'small village hunting' which was reasonably successful and did some shopping (!). All a bit dusty and horse shitty and would have killed for a beer but no usable toilet anywhere. Transylvania is so very poor, most villagers just manage to survive in the way they always have, hand to mouth. We despair as to the future of this mostly spectacular region.

We seem to have a hockey team celebrating about 3 feet from our hotel window tonight – our most valiant translation of their songs is "Go Csikszerada we are the best, we are the hockey/footy/soccer champs and fuck all the rest". It'll be close......... Kate has a better version: " We beated the other team; we smoted them with our hockey sticks until they bled from their eyes; God bless the hockey field; God bless the line markers; God bless those who maked the goalnets; We owe everything to our Roman forefathers; Oh..and a little bit to our Dacian foremothers; God bless Romania; All things are possible in Romania; We shall return next week when we smite our enemy again".

In the morning Istvan informed us that it was, in fact, a wedding.

""**Sfantu Gheorge** (*Sepsiszentgyorgy*)

Szekely Museum"

This was a fantastic museum – even made a murmured mention of the nobility. As Kate says "we totally support all overthrowing of the ruling class but for goodness' sake try and do something that's a bit better" – that hasn't happened yet – we think the peasants may be worse off and there's probably more of 'em now than there were 100 years ago, as a percentage of the population.

We also trudged around a cemetery and found lots of Szekely tombs and grave poles amongst, about, outside and inside an ever present ancient citadel.

Big day so also Harman fortress (citadel) which did not house a single dynasty but rather lots of peasants so there were lots of possibly charming little separate living quarters for possibly peasants.

Highlight of the day was Bran Castle, home of Queen Marie of Romania, grandaughter of Queen Victoria (soooo inbred, these Royal families). Similar to Neuschwanstein in location and appearance, it has thousands of small comfy rooms up and down the most astonishing staircases, small, big, medium, tiny and miniscule. We must have walked up at least 2,000 steps today. And yesterday was 20 degrees (too hot, needed aircon) whereas today was 2 degrees, raining and snowing (just like

Tassie really). But a castle in the snow is a thing of beauty and this castle was well worth all the dripping, freezing effort.

Thence to
"**Brasov** (*Brasso*)

Heart and hub of Transylvania a 13thC Saxon rich town still largely surrounded by medieval stone walls is only hours away from castles, villages and mountains. One of the main attractions is the 14thC Black Church which is the largest Gothic church between Vienna and Istanbul. 120fabulous antique Turkish rugs adorn the walls – gifts from merchants over the centuries. It also has a 4,000 pipe church organ. About 5,000 black and brown bears live in Romania and many have started relocating to Brasov....."

We had some small touristy spack attacks here as our hotel was rubbish (even Istvan thought so) so relocated a few times until we were happy and ended up at Bella Muzica which is GREAT (although we did pay many extra Lei to get a suite) and had speccy and tasty food for dinner – the best we have had so far in our whole trip.....Shouted Istvan to a meal as a gesture of real and undying gratitude and we had a very merry evening.

Went walking in the snow in Brasov – well actually it was cold but quite nice. Saw many towers (Weavers Tower, Horseshoe Makers Tower, Peopleshoe Makers Tower, Goldsmiths Tower etc – something like that anyway). Black Church terrific but persian rugs were all placed too high up for a bit of lightfingeredness damn it. Saw the narrowest street in Europe and tried to pay $30 for something which actually only cost $3 – much gay girlish laughter from shop staff. Narrowly avoided all the bears. The Tourist Bureau, door open, sign placed outside saying it was open, fully staffed and heated announced that it was closed when we walked in – you learn not to argue.

Sending this off now – an afternoon's chore as for some reason can only send to 10 multiple recipients at a time. The next email will be about Bucharest (we suspect BIG YUKKY city) and Miklósvár (we suspect most gorgeous small village in the entire world with Welcome Home Shirley on a big banner).

Lots of love from Transylvania.

Dear family and friends: For those of you who don't remember we will be home on 12th April (late in the day).

Drove from Brasov and decided to spend two hours exploring the sun and the moon and the sky and the veritable heavens – went right UP into the Bucegi Mountains, including a cable car to take us as high as possible, "only" 2,000m but it was extraordinary and magnificent, a mountain which gazed out on a much higher complete mountain range which surrounded us and gleamed very brightly and insistently with unending snow. And there were bear and wolf warning signs so we felt lucky to escape with our lives. Treading in the footsteps of the gods of Olympus. Imagine Heaven with cable car and you come close but of course then there are the wonderful signature conifers which define this region so uniquely. But they are just on the way up and give way to pure white everywhere on all the summits.

It was one of the best things we have done in Transylvania. And yes it's when we have to stop trying to be funny and start trying to be poetic that words fail us!

Then to

"Bucharest

Palace of the Parliament (second largest building in the world) and The Village Museum of the Romanian Peasant"

Bucharest is as traffic sodden and insane as we thought it would be but much prettier than expected. Unexpectedly we rather like it. It is raucous and lively and energetic, somewhat reminiscent of New York City. The main attraction so far has been watching the traffic from our hotel window. Inexplicably, policemen pop out and start directing traffic even though there are traffic lights, so drivers can SEE that the light is green but the policeman has overridden this, leading to even greater frustration by the already psychotic drivers. When we first stepped outside the door of our (very nice) hotel, after having sent Istvan home to his wife, we noticed that the trolley bus wires were smoking, as far as we could see in both directions, and not just smoking, but sizzling and imminently alight. There was a deep smoky, smelly haze which made us fear for the immediate future of our hotel. Romanians seemed unfazed but were taking photos so it was clearly not a usual thing to happen. We THINK it was the trolley bus wires but, given that there are great garlands and bunches of wires hanging everywhere in impenetrable bundles, it could have been anything. Thence to our Lonely Planet recommended restaurant where we had a pork chop, cabbage and the best chips we've ever tasted. The restaurant itself had far too much really big furniture stuffed into it, so every time someone needed to move or get to a table, the whole restaurant had to stand up, push and pull their chairs around, rather like one of those puzzle games where you have to make a picture by sliding little cubes into place. And there was also a VERY drunk man who was itching for a fight so we ate rather quickly before he decided that Australians were a suitable target and inched our way out (excuse me, excuse me).

A note on Romanian hotels – they are really very good and for somewhere between $15 and $50 you can upgrade to a suite which we have done consistently for the past ten days. However we HAVE finally arrived in a hotel with a magnifying makeup mirror and, to our horror, have discovered bristles abounding. Istvan should have warned us that we were slowly turning into werewolves in the back seat.

Now back to the traffic! We were quite convinced that the overnight noise from the street indicated that Bucharest was being slowly demolished, to be quickly rebuilt before morning, so got out of bed to do more traffic watching. Found that the road was being re-tarmaced the old fashioned way, lots of large machinery but mainly people on picks and shovels. In the morning decided that the road didn't look much different.

Today went PAST the Palace of the President – refused to go on a guided tour on principle (the principle being mainly that it looked exhausting) then to the Museum of the Peasant which is described as heartbreakingly sweet (Lonely Planet) and won a prize for being the best small museum in Europe some years ago. It was excellent, did not break our hearts but was a good farewell to Romanian museums. And it wasn't all that small so little tired feet found a French bakery for lunch and had toasted ham, cheese and tomato baguettes which were a somewhat welcome change from Romanian food – especially given that we will have to eat a lot of it in the next five days....Did find the most terrific little church on the way home which was squished in between large bland buildings – an oasis.

Had to get up very early this morning to go to Miklósvár – only 4 hours travel time on Australian roads but will take at least 10 hours (not kidding). Looked out the window and saw our first pack of wild dogs. Infamous in Bucharest, they descended from Communist era guard dogs and many are rabid! Glad we were inside.

Set off at 8am for

Miclosoara (*Miklósvár*)

By 9am we were still stuck in Bucharest traffic! Stopped off at the completely over the top Peles Palace, gross Germanic gloomy 'splendour' (which Queen Marie reportedly loathed) in Sinaia and the much lovelier, much smaller Pelisor Palace which was as cosy as a castle can possibly get. Lunched, saw two bears and a wolf (well, they had been dead for some time and adorned the walls of our restaurant), whipped back around Brasov and then onto the muddy, rutted tracks leading to Miklósvár. Rather emotional but settled in to our 'Kalnoky guest house' which is small but very sweet and then went for a short stroll through part of the village – it's not that big but it was pretty cold and a storm seemed to be brewing.

Dinner at 8!! (Breakfast at 9!!; Lunch at 2!!) Yikes. Survived till dinner by putting watches back, a pathetic psychological ploy usually employed to placate children. Communal eating but only four other guests and all quite jolly, although Kate stole wine from one of them – oh well he was Swedish. Lamingtons for dessert. If they were trying to cook an Australian dish dunno why they didn't do vegemite on toast which would have been more than welcome.

Best sleep. After the extremely late breakfast we decided to immerse ourselves in the countryside and went for a five hour horse and cart ride which was just great. Very misty morning which gave way to beautiful mountainous vistas and rolling green hills with amazing oak, beech, hornbeam forests, some conifers. Also Spring is springing and wildflowers are already beautifying the woodlands, violets and hellebores. Adventures to be had along the way included befurring of all outer garments by horsehair and runaway horse and cart (once without us and once with us – no driver, Shirley nearly fell completely out). Hugely muddy. All grew about 18 inches taller from the amount of mud on our shoes. Nice pork chop barbecue and stroll in the forest. Kate went on another stroll to view mother boar with babies while Shirley cried in the forest (she's done a bit of that....)

Tomorrow we have a Meeting with the Priest to talk about parish records (with a translator) and then might knock on doors to chat to "Cousins".

Have solved first mystery as to the real origin of the Szekely – firmly believe that they are descendants of the Uigar tribes in China or they could have been from Scotland. Anyone who disputes either of these theories better have some good evidence.

Visited local cemetery today and took photos of all Gyenge graves. That filled in the time before lunch which was three courses – we hope to be able to fit into our clothes by the time we leave here as ALL meals are three courses. Or, as Kate says, we hope to be able to still fit into our clothes by dinner time. Then waddled to the priest's house with our translator. The priest was very efficient, had all records dating back about a zillion years and no record at all of grandparent's marriage, mother's birth or indeed anything at all. Made generous donation to the church and wandered down the road to our nearest cousin. This was equally uninformative (and also very hot as all heaters ablaze) but wife popped down the road to get the local retired schoolteacher who turned out to be somewhat more than a trifle affected with Alzheimers but chatted amiably enough about HER family tree. Before we could leave we were confronted with a crock'n'bush of what seemed to be lamingtons again which strained our clothing even further. Then, in an ever growing parade of people, husband, translator and we two popped down another road to visit his sister (also very hot house). All agog, the whole family also knew nothing but by then Shirley's forebears were being not so indirectly accused of being NOT REALLY CATHOLICS as otherwise they would be instantly known to all. No lamingtons thank goodness but we are invited back tomorrow because some other cousin is driving at breakneck speed with a Family Tree of whatever family it is we are actually talking about by now....

Everyone agreed, to a man and woman and cousin, that there had never been any other 'big house' in the village.

There was some mention that maybe the main guesthouse where we are staying could maybe have been their house because it is the biggest house in the village. ALL, to a man and woman, ignored the elephant in the room as in the 16thC so called hunting manor next door (well, in its own park) which is huge and fits every description ever given to Shirley by mother or grandmother. So we cunningly conceded to our translator, who after all works for Count Kalnoky, the supposed traditional owner of the manor, that, yes, the guesthouse is most likely it and then went to visit the manor. In all Shirley's attempts at descriptions of her family's home, she said it was a keep or fortified manor house. Everyone denies that there ever has been anything like a keep in the village. So it was an interesting slip of the tongue when we were actually inside the Big House for the translator to take us down to the cellars and point out where the 'keep' or fortified area used to be...... Kalnoky's website also claims that, after a long dispute the Romanians finally allowed him to reclaim his ancestral hunting manor. Our translator told us that he actually only has it on a 99 year lease. The house itself is very very large and in extremely bad repair but it was easy to imagine what it would have looked like, fully furnished and buzzing with warmth and light and laughter. We will go back tomorrow by ourselves and explore the grounds which are still extensive and have rather lovely trees, almost woodlands. Shirley will be looking for the remains of a three person outside dunny which her mother remembered. If this is found it will be Bingo! time. Yes, it's come down to this as the final proof!

During all the trudging around we also trudged back to the chapel in the cemetery as our translator had the keys. Jeez, talk about "spin". The chapel had been completely gutted except for three recently painted watercolours of the various versions of the Kalnoky coat of arms. NB There were no Kalnokys in the cemetery.

Tomorrow we also plan to paint eggs and go to church, yes church. Easter Sunday in Miklósvár! However not really sure whether we should go to the Catholic church or the Calvinist one.............

We think that the whole village might be talking about us by now.

Dear family and friends

This is our final blog, a record of a sometimes exhausting, sometimes emotional, but amazingly fascinating and exciting trip.

We are pleased to report BINGO!!!! Found the ultimate proof of ownership, the three person outside dunny! A quite stunning moment really, to walk towards an unassuming little broken down building at the rear of the castle, thinking No Way could this be it, enter through the single doorway to find three old stone cubicles probably dating from the late 19thC with holes in the relevant places.

Then proceeded to examine every blade of grass, every flower and every branch of every tree in the "park" and every room, stone, niche, doorway, beam and brick inside the building. Took about 3 million photos (you poor things) and felt at last as though we had Walked the Land. Kate was also molested by a horse.

In the afternoon went back to one of the Cousins and met with a young cousin who spoke English (bliss) and had, not a family tree, but some good information about websites. We tried desperately to get rid of our minder/translator but he refused to budge so we were unable to speak as frankly as we would have wished. Exchanged email addresses and will have frank exchanges via email as soon as we are able. As it were.

Sitting writing this in the main area of the guesthouse and someone rudely interrupted us – turned out to be the Count offering tea. We declined. On the way back from the cousins we told the minder/translator that Shirley was the true owner of the castle (yes, it's a castle now! It actually is – not kidding, wait for photos). Can't wait for him to tell Count Tibor – could be an interesting evening.

Evening: No, not interesting as the Count disappeared right after his brief royal appearance

– a relief really as otherwise the men in sunglasses and big black cars would have been on the doorstep next morning.

Continued to have a lovely pleasant peasant experience all next day. Freezing cold again so just ate heaps (including crepes although we had sworn off dessert, irresistible) and lounged around.

Off to Brasov train station on Easter Tuesday with our driver Jozsef who turned out to be another cousin – it's a small world. Shirley said goodbye to her mother as she had finally taken her back home to her beloved Miklósvár. Decided Miklósvár countryside looked a little bit like Tasmania so there will always be Tasmania to remind her.

On train to Vienna. Had booked first class sleeping compartments for our 15 hour journey so reasonably relaxed about it all. Searched desperately for our little bathroom but it wasn't there for some reason so resigned to using communal shower in the morning (more of that later!). Restaurant car ok and had been given some sort of voucher by the conductor for our breakfast so hopped into our little bunks for a good long sleep. HA HA. Woken up four times during the night by Romanian passport control, a conductor to check tickets, Hungarian passport control, then a conductor telling us our door was unlocked. Very little sleep was, in fact, had. Shower turned out to only have cold water so a quick sluice then an attempt to dry ourselves using the paper hankies which posed as 'towels' in our sleeping car kit. Ended up using the microfibre towels given as gift before we left. Thank you Barb and Ruve! Then off to breakfast. Raced through the many train carriages but unfortunately came to a premature stop as we realised that the restaurant car had mysteriously dropped off. Oh right, the vouchers were meant to be exchanged for a breakfast package the night before. Intrepid travellers that we are, we ate the coloured Easter eggs which had been given to us by Betty and Zoli (new friends made in Miklósvár) and then fantasised about coffee for the next 3 hours until we got to Vienna.

Already filthy (and singularly blithely unworried about this) we bussed off to Vienna airport and embarked for our flights to Dubai and then to Bangkok. Usual ghastly plane travel experience so arrived in Bangkok to 37 degree heat a great deal filthier than we had been 20 hours earlier. Jumped into our limousine with liveried driver and off to The Mandarin Oriental for our 'suite' experience. Whether it was just general decrepitude or complete overtiredness we immediately agreed to some sort of upgrade (we will never tell anyone what we ended up paying!) and zoomed up to the top floor where we found probably the best view in Bangkok from all 38 of our windows, spent the next two hours being sightseers in our accommodation, then room service (not a single bottle of wine costing less than $100 – bemoaned the loss of our $3 Romanian wines) and to bed in 8 foot square white pillowy bliss for about 12 hours uninterrupted sleep at last. Called it LOLLOL = Lap of Luxury Laugh out Loud.

Couldn't find the elephant in the room.

Breakfast the next morning was outdoors right on the river. Kate visibly flinched as we left the hotel aircon but survived right through to the third coffee nevertheless. It seems as though we then spent some hours being sightseers in our hotel which is quite probably the best hotel in the world (it actually has consistently won awards saying this very thing) as it combines history with taste, elegance and utter comfort and luxury. Even the new wings have extensively mirrored some of the best features of the original hotel, including cunningly situated louvred windows but not, thank goodness, ceiling fans for cooling.

Having finished being sightseers in our accommodation and our hotel we ventured out to do SHOPPING. Yes, shopping. Two go mad in Bangkok.

After sober lunch of tropical/exotic fruit did a tour of the Grand Palace. Our guide informed us that April was the hottest month to be in Bangkok and that this year the hot was hotter than usual – 40 degrees. And a lot of walking. And very little shade. Even the shade was hot. At least we have stopped whining about the extreme cold..... The Grand Palace was, however, extraordinary. It is a 'Wat' which means, apart from the Inner Palace where the royal family lives, a temple complex which includes the Emerald Buddha temple, even more gilded than Romanian Orthodox churches. Not that that means anything to youse out there in bloggee land but WE know wat we mean.

Even our Thai guide was hot. So we left a bit early! Came back via a circuitous route in order to avoid the red shirt protesters which we were a bit glad of as, apparently, traffic can be held up for hours. Keep on getting "message from management" in our sweet suite telling Dear Tourist, not to worry" soothe soothe. Hey do we look worried?

Popped across the river on one of the Oriental's complimentary boats (just because we could) then came back and had espresso from our own machine, showered AGAIN and ordered a massively over priced Aussie red for a pre dinner drinkie. Every time we leave our room, no matter how briefly, someone comes in and does things – replaces towels (we already have about ten), washes cups and glasses (have multiples of these, they must think we're about to have a party), brings more fruit (already have enough to save Captain Cook's entire fleet from scurvy), adds extra toiletries (have seven different kinds of shampoo and spare French soap in a little soap cupboard). Kate got about four different messages about her clean laundry, sort of like a Hansel and Gretel crumb trail to the 'dressing room'. And then there are the discarded clothes left on the floor –still dirty but beautifully folded. Princess Shirley wants to live here permanently.

Overdid it last night – massively overpriced wine bill could probably solve Greece's debt crisis but it was the second last night so....

Took a longtail boat this morning to visit a floating market, the Royal Barge factory and some of the small klongs to view remaining bits of old Bangkok canal living. It blew the cobwebs out after last night! It was fun – Ratty and Moley kind of revisited. Then found we were able to purchase panadol and aspirin from hotel so should be right for the rest of the day. Getting really lazy and starting to see the attraction of what most people in the hotel seem to do, which is get up, have breakfast, lie by the pool, have drinks brought, have lunch, lie by the pool, have drinks brought, have dinner, go to bed. Compared to them we look like quite adventurous tourists.

Not much time left in Bangkok – hope the protesters don't block the road to the airport tomorrow. If they do we will either have to get a bank loan or move to the YWCA.

Sending off – probably just lie by the pool and have drinks brought for the rest of our stay.

Lots of love from Shirley and Kate

9. Hobart: A Farewell too hard to bear

This small piece of strange family history was largely written for the same reason we went off to Transylvania to search for my mother's past. It was a way of not saying goodbye to her. She died in 2007 and, although her love and character fills me every minute of every day, I refuse to say that last goodbye. I took her home to Miklósvár and so there I must go again if only to touch the stones that warmed her childhood and all of her memories of happiness. She was fond of the phrase 'One eye laughing, one eye crying'. She felt that it summed up life itself.

Eva and Charles in Launceston around 1963

Eva and father in Nagyvarad around 1935-6

Eva in Nagyvarad around 1937

Me aged about 2

Eva and her mother in Australia after the war

www.ingramcontent.com/pod-product-compliance
Lightning Source LLC
Chambersburg PA
CBHW071143160426
43196CB00011B/1994